Dying and Rising with Christ

THE THEOLOGY OF PAUL THE APOSTLE

Terrance Callan

Paulist Press
New York/Mahwah, N.J.

Cover design by Cynthia Dunne
Book design by Lynn Else

Library of Congress Cataloging-in-Publication Data

Callan Terrance, 1947-
    Dying and rising with Christ : the theology of Paul the Apostle / Terrance Callan.
        p. cm.
    Includes bibliographical references (p.   ).
    ISBN 0-8091-4395-X (alk. paper)
    1. Bible. N.T. Epistles of Paul—Theology. 2. Paul, the Apostle, Saint. 3. Jesus Christ—Person and offices. I. Title.
    BS2651.C28 2006
    227'.06—dc22

                                                                    2006002750

Published by Paulist Press
997 Macarthur Boulevard
Mahwah, New Jersey, 07430

www.paulistpress.com

Printed and bound in the
United States of America

CONTENTS

Contents

CONTENTS

Contents

INTRODUCTION

Theology can be defined as thought about God, especially systematic thought about God, and all that is involved in, and follows directly from, such thought. As the title of this book indicates, the apostle Paul believed that an understanding of Christ was involved in, and followed directly from, thought about God. Further, Paul saw the believer's union with Christ in his death and resurrection as central to the significance of Christ.

Along with the Gospel according to John, the letters of Paul express the most profound and comprehensive theological vision to be found in the New Testament. This vision has had enormous influence on subsequent Christian thought and indirectly on Western thought in general. Nevertheless, there are aspects of this vision that have been overlooked, forgotten, or set aside in the course of time. Thus these aspects are new to contemporary believers and can renew their understanding of Christianity.

For Christians, the letters of Paul, along with the rest of the Bible, are God's revelation and thus authoritative for Christian belief and behavior. For good reason, many Christians find Paul's letters difficult to comprehend. The description of Paul's theology that follows should help readers understand the letters, each of which expresses only the aspects of Paul's theological vision that serve the specific purpose of the letter. In addition the presentation of Paul's general theological vision should help readers see more clearly what Paul's letters imply for Christian life today.

Problems

The attempt to describe Paul's theology immediately encounters two problems. The first is that there is significant disagreement among scholars of the New Testament as to how many genuine writings of Paul we possess. Thirteen letters of Paul have been preserved in the New Testament. Most New Testament scholars, however, doubt that Paul wrote all thirteen. There is general agreement that Paul wrote Romans, 1 and 2 Corinthians, Galatians, Philippians, 1 Thessalonians, and Philemon. Varying degrees of doubt attach to the authenticity of the others. Although most scholars doubt that Paul wrote Ephesians, Colossians, and 2 Thessalonians,[1] I myself consider the case against their authenticity unproved. I agree, however, with the overwhelming majority of scholars that Paul probably did not write 1 and 2 Timothy and Titus.[2]

In the following account of the theology of Paul, I will presume that the undoubted letters provide reliable information about Paul's theology. I will also make use of information from Ephesians, Colossians, and 2 Thessalonians, though acknowledging the existence of serious doubts that in these letters Paul himself is speaking. And I will presume that 1 and 2 Timothy and Titus do not derive from Paul himself, though they may also contain reliable information about his theology.

After the letters of Paul, the best source of information about Paul is the Acts of the Apostles, which includes an extensive presentation of Paul's career. It is generally agreed, however, that the presentation of Paul's theology in Acts does not conform very closely to the information provided by Paul's own letters.[3] Because of this my reconstruction of Paul's theology comes entirely from his letters, and I make use of Acts only insofar as it is compatible with this reconstruction.

The second problem we encounter as we attempt to present Paul's theology is that Paul did not write his letters in order to present his theological outlook. Each of them was written to a specific

---

1. See W. G. Kümmel, *Introduction*, 357–63 (Ephesians), 340–46 (Colossians), 264–69 (2 Thessalonians). Kümmel himself argues for the authenticity of Colossians and 2 Thessalonians. (Full Publication information for modern works cited in the footnotes appears in the bibliography.)

2. Ibid., 370–84. J. Murphy-O'Connor argues that 2 Timothy is authentic (*Paul: A Critical Life*, 357–59).

3. P. Vielhauer, "On the 'Paulinism' of Acts," in W. A. Meeks, ed., *The Writings of St. Paul*, 166–75.

group of Christians[4] to discuss the particular problems facing them. In doing this, Paul refers to many theological matters, but his purpose is not to present his theology but rather to bring these theological matters to bear on the situation of those to whom he writes. At a high level of generality, two main themes can be discerned in Paul's letters:

1. Eschatology and its implications for Christian life—this is the theme of 1 and 2 Thessalonians and 1 and 2 Corinthians
2. The relationship between the Christian church and Israel—this is the theme of Galatians, Philippians, Romans, and Ephesians

One point confirming that these are the main themes of Paul's letters is that his earliest interpreters saw them as his main themes.

The Understanding of Paul by His Earliest Interpreters

Wayne Meeks summarizes the views of Paul's earliest interpreters under four headings:[5]

1. Paul as Satan's apostle: Jewish Christian opponents
2. The only true Apostle: Marcion's radical Paul
3. The model ascetic
4. The domesticated apostle

The first three views are those of heretics; the last is that of the church fathers. Views 1 and 2 both perceive Paul's main message as opposition to the Jewish law, which is one of the main topics in Paul's discussion of the relationship between the Christian

---

4. Despite the note in Acts 11:26 that the followers of Jesus were first called Christians in Antioch, it is clear that referring to Paul and his contemporary followers of Jesus as Christians is anachronistic. Paul never uses this term, and Acts does not use it apart from the passage just mentioned. It remains, however, a convenient way to refer to the followers of Jesus, and I will make use of it.

5. Meeks, *The Writings of St. Paul*, 176–213.

church and Israel. Because Paul argued against the law, his Jewish Christian opponents regarded him as Satan's apostle and rejected him. For Marcion (ca. 85–160), Paul's argument against the law made Paul the only true apostle. Marcion thought that Paul's rejection of the law implied rejection of the Jewish scriptures and of the God revealed in them.

One example of rejection of Paul by his Jewish Christian opponents is found in the writings of the church father Epiphanius (ca. 315–403). Epiphanius says that the Ebionites, one group of Jewish Christians, reject Paul by attacking his motives for arguing against the law.

> They declare that he was a Greek, child of a Greek mother and a Greek father. He went up to Jerusalem, they say, and when he had spent some time there, he was seized with a passion to marry a daughter of the priest. For this reason he became a proselyte and was circumcised. Then, when he failed to get the girl, he flew into a rage and wrote against circumcision and against Sabbath and Law.[6]

By indicating that Paul's opposition to the law derived from this experience, the Ebionites attempt to show that this opposition has no validity. Of course, they are mistaken in saying that Paul was a Gentile who converted to Judaism, so this argument is entirely without merit.

Adolf von Harnack describes the starting point for Marcion's thoroughgoing rejection of Judaism in this way:

> It lay in the Pauline opposition of Law and Gospel—on the one side malicious, narrow and vindictive justice; on the other, merciful love. Marcion immersed himself in the basic thought of the Letters to Galatians and Romans, and in them he discovered the full explanation of the nature of Christianity, the Old Testament and the world.[7]

Marcion correctly perceived that Paul saw tension between law and gospel, but he misunderstood the nature of that tension. Paul believed

---

6. Ibid., 177–78.
7. Ibid., 190–91.

that one and the same God both gave the law and sent Jesus; consequently, there is no fundamental opposition between them even though the law has now come to an end.

The third view identified by Meeks perceives Paul as maintaining that Christians must be ascetics; this is one topic in Paul's discussion of eschatology and its implications for Christian life. More specifically, proponents of this view argued that to be a Christian required complete sexual abstinence—celibacy for those not married and cessation of sexual intercourse by those already married. An example of this view can be found in Tatian's (ca. 110–80) comment on 1 Cor 7:5.

> While agreement to be continent makes prayer possible, intercourse of corruption destroys it. By the very disparaging way he [Paul] allows it, he forbids it. For although he allowed them to come together again because of Satan and the temptation to incontinence, he indicated that the man who takes advantage of this permission will be serving two masters, God if there is "agreement," but, if there is no such agreement, incontinence, fornication and the devil.[8]

What Tatian thinks Paul said in 1 Cor 7:5 is exactly the opposite of what he did say. Paul is actually urging married Corinthians to have sexual intercourse with one another.

The fourth view identified by Meeks, that of the church fathers, is partly a rejection of the other three views. This is a "domesticated" interpretation of Paul that sees him at home among orthodox Christians rather than heretics. In reaction to the first two views, and especially that of Marcion, the church fathers emphasized Paul's positive attitude toward the law. They did this in two ways. First, they stressed the educational function of the law as a pedagogue preparing people for the coming of Christ. Second, they introduced a distinction between moral and ceremonial law, arguing that Paul rejected the latter but not the former. The church fathers rejected the ascetical interpretation of Paul by correctly insisting on the moral rather than physical meaning of the word "flesh" for Paul.

---

8. Ibid., 195.

The church fathers also reflected on other themes in Paul's letters under the influence of their own circumstances. They tended to interpret Paul's language about the person of Christ as explicitly indicating details of the beliefs formulated at the councils of Nicaea (325) and Chalcedon (451). Their reflections on grace, faith, and works did not reckon with the original context of Paul's discussion of them, that is, his discussion of the relationship between the Christian church and Israel. Instead Paul's statements on these topics were interpreted in light of other New Testament passages or the experience of the church.

Method

All of this makes it clear that Paul himself did not formulate a systematic statement of his theology in his letters. How, then, can we formulate such a statement on the basis of his letters?

1. We have noted above that as Paul discusses the various topics of his letters, he makes frequent reference to theological matters. The first step is to gather together all of Paul's references to a given theological matter and try to discern Paul's view of that matter. Since Paul refers to these matters as he speaks to the problems confronting his churches, the various references are not always obviously consistent with one another. This is especially true of matters Paul discusses frequently, such as the Jewish law. It is generally possible, however, to discover a consistent view underlying the references.

2. The second step is to arrange the various theological matters in some coherent pattern. At this point there is danger of imposing an alien structure on Paul's thought. In order to minimize this danger, we will use the outline of Paul's Letter to the Romans as far as possible. Romans is Paul's longest and most systematic letter. Although it is addressed to a specific situation, it is as close as Paul comes to a systematic exposition of his thought. Others who have attempted to present Paul's theology have also relied on Romans, though the results vary considerably. In the fol-

lowing presentation, nine theological topics will be discussed in the following order. In the cases where Paul discusses the topic extensively within his Letter to the Romans, that passage will also be discussed. The topics are:

I. God
II. Humanity apart from Christ—Romans 1:18–3:20
III. Salvation
   A. Salvation as a free gift—Romans 3:21–4:25
   B. The person of Christ (Christology)
   C. The action of Christ (soteriology)—Romans 5:12—6:11; 7:1–4
   D. Salvation as death with Christ to sin—Romans 7
   E. Salvation as new life with Christ—Romans 8; 9–11
   F. Humanity in Christ: baptism, Eucharist, church, sex and marriage
IV. Ethics—Romans 12:1–15:13

As the citations from Romans suggest, most of these topics and their arrangement derive from the Letter to the Romans. The exceptions are God, the person of Christ, and humanity in Christ. Since theology is thought about God, it makes sense to begin with Paul's ideas about God, even though Paul himself does not discuss this topic at any length. Perhaps because of this, the topic has often not received much attention from those who have described Paul's theology. It then makes sense to discuss the situation from which the human race needed salvation in Paul's view, and this is the way Paul begins his presentation in Romans. After describing the need for salvation, it then makes sense to discuss Paul's understanding of how salvation is accomplished. Most of the remainder of this description of Paul's theology is concerned with various aspects of salvation's accomplishment. One salient characteristic of salvation as Paul understands it is that it is a free gift of God accepted by faith. I begin by discussing this because it is the point Paul makes in Romans immediately after he presents the need for salvation. The agent of salvation is Christ. So I proceed to discuss Paul's understanding of who Christ is and how he accomplishes salvation; Paul discusses the latter in Romans after arguing that salvation is a free gift. Continuing to follow the order of Paul's presentation in Romans, I proceed to discuss salvation as death with Christ to sin, setting the human race free from sin, and salvation as new life into which the human race has entered through the action of Christ. The latter I divide into present and future new life. Finally I discuss the incorporation of the human race into Christ, the most important way of speaking about new life with Christ. The final topic is ethics. Paul discusses this at the end of Romans and many of his other letters.

One might use this same procedure to formulate the systematic theology of a preacher on the basis of a collection of sermons. The formulation that results will be different from any of the materials on which it is based and something the author of those materials might not affirm in every detail. It may confront us with inconsistencies in the references to a single topic and gaps in the way we arrange them. Our ability to resolve the inconsistencies and fill the gaps may be limited. This is partly because the inconsistencies and gaps only come to light in the attempt to formulate a systematic theology, something the author did not do.

The Central Theme of Paul's Theology

What is most distinctive about this presentation of Paul's theology is the argument that dying and rising with Christ as part of the body of Christ is central both to Paul's understanding of Jesus as Savior and to his understanding of Christian life. Others have perceived the importance Paul assigns to dying and rising with Christ and belonging to the body of Christ; they are noted in the following discussion. This is, however, the only presentation of Paul's theology as a whole that sees its central theme as dying and rising with Christ as part of the body of Christ. The closest parallel is Albert Schweitzer's *Mysticism of Paul the Apostle*, a thorough exploration of Paul's "mysticism," which is Schweitzer's name for what I see as the central theme of Paul's theology. Schweitzer does not, however, attempt to describe Paul's theology itself.

In his book Schweitzer criticizes attempts to explain Paul's derivation of this central theme from Hellenistic mystery religions or from his conversion experience.[9] Instead Schweitzer argues that Paul based his view on the eschatological expectation that the elect would have solidarity with one another and with the Messiah, a solidarity brought into being by the death and resurrection of Jesus before full arrival of the end.[10]

I am inclined to think Paul may have come to this view on the basis of his conversion experience, though not in the way that Schweitzer rejects. According to the Acts of the Apostles, Paul was on his way to Damascus to persecute Christians when a voice asked him, "Saul, Saul, why do you persecute me?" Paul asked, "Who are you, Lord?" and the voice replied, "I am Jesus, whom you are persecuting" (Acts 9:1–5).[11] It would be very natural for Paul to conclude from this that Jesus identified himself with those who followed him, that in some sense his followers were Jesus. And Paul could have inferred from this identification that Christians die and rise with Christ as part of the body of Christ.[12]

In his letters Paul himself does not describe his encounter with the risen Christ the same way it is described in Acts. For a number of reasons, however, it is entirely plausible that Acts is correct in saying that such a dialogue between Jesus and Paul was part of Paul's conversion. First, apart from something like this dialogue, it seems hard to explain how Paul would have known who it was that had appeared to him. Since Paul had not previously seen Jesus, he would not have been able to identify him by sight alone. Second, the identification of Jesus with his followers implied by the dialogue plays no important role in Acts' presentation of Paul. This makes it unlikely that it has been introduced into the story for some theological purpose of Acts. Third, although Paul does not mention such a dialogue in his letters, nothing in the letters precludes such a dialogue's having been part of his vision of Christ. Thus the dialogue may be historical.

---

9. A. Schweitzer, *Mysticism of Paul*, 26–40.

10. Ibid., 75–140, esp. 113.

11. See also Acts 22:5–8; 26:9–15.

12. For this view, see J. A. T. Robinson, *The Body*, 55–58. J. D. G. Dunn rejects this idea (*Theology of Paul*, 549).

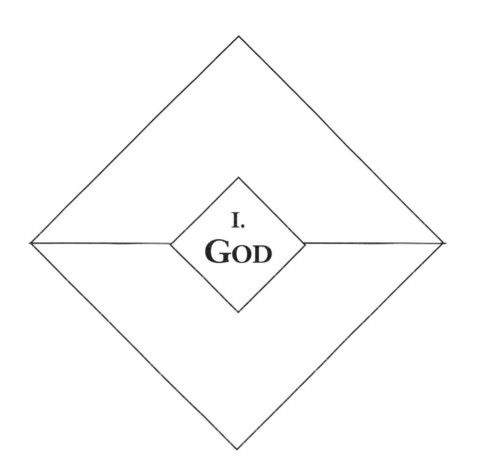

I.

GOD

We begin our exploration of the theology of Paul by discussing Paul's understanding of God, his theology in the strictest sense.[1] God is mentioned very frequently in the letters of Paul (548 times), but Paul never expounds at length an understanding of God. For the most part, he seems to presume that he and his readers have the same understanding of God.

The following presentation is divided into four parts. The first describes how Paul sees God in himself; the second, how Paul sees God in relation to others; and the third, how Paul thinks human beings should relate to God; the fourth makes some summary observations on the picture of God that emerges from the first three. The first three topics are closely interrelated. This is especially true of the first and second, since the characteristics of God in himself are most often revealed in God's interaction with others.

God in Himself

Paul's letters refer to a number of qualities of God. We will discuss seven qualities or groups of qualities.

1. God Is One

Paul says in 1 Cor 8:4,

There is no God but one.

Paul also mentions this central article of Jewish faith in other places.[2] In Rom 3:29–30 Paul argues that God is God of both Jew and Gentile because God is one. In 1 Cor 8:6 he argues that all others recognized by some as gods are so-called gods (v. 5), idols who have no real existence (v. 4). He also makes the latter point by speak-

---

1. On Paul's view of God, see J. A. Fitzmyer, "Pauline Teaching," 104–10; Dunn, *Theology of Paul*, 28–50.

2. Rom 3:30; 1 Cor 8:6; Gal 3:20; Eph 4:6; cf. 1 Tim 2:5. On this topic, see G. F. Moore, *Judaism*, 1:360–67; Meeks, *First Urban Christians*, 165–70.

ing of God as the only God (Rom 16:27; cf. 1 Tim 1:17) and the true God (1 Thess 1:9) and by referring to the gods recognized by other people as those not by nature gods (Gal 4:8), idols whom Christians have abandoned (1 Thess 1:9), and so-called gods (2 Thess 2:4).

Paul's monotheism is qualified in two ways. First, alongside the one God is the one Lord Jesus Christ (1 Cor 8:6; Eph 4:5); cf. also the reference to Jesus as the one mediator between God and humankind in 1 Tim 2:5. Paul does not make it clear in these passages how he understands the relationship between the two. We will discuss this further below in "The Person of Christ."

The second qualification of Paul's monotheism is that he seems to see a reality underlying the gods worshiped by others. In 1 Cor 10:19–20 Paul expressly denies that an idol is anything, yet he asserts that sacrifices offered to them are offered to demons, not to God, and are able to unite with the demons the one offering the sacrifice. This is a reason Christians should not participate in these sacrifices.

> What pagans sacrifice, they sacrifice to demons and not to God. I do not want you to be partners with demons.
>
> (1 Cor 10:20)

The idea that there are other spiritual powers in the universe, at least somewhat hostile to God, probably underlies Paul's reference to the god of this world in 2 Cor 4:4. Paul more commonly refers to these powers under the names "ruler" (ἀρχή[3] or ἄρχων[4]), "power" (δύναμις),[5] "authority" (ἐξουσία),[6] etc.[7]

2. God Is Living

Paul refers to God as living in Rom 9:26 (quoting Hos 1:10 [LXX 2:1]) and several other places[8] and once presents God as saying "I live" (Rom 14:11). In addition to the passage from Hosea,

---

3. Rom 8:38; 1 Cor 15:24; Eph 1:21; 3:10; 6:12; Col 1:16; 2:10, 15.
4. 1 Cor 2:6, 8; Eph 2:2.
5. Rom 8:38; 1 Cor 15:24; Eph 1:21.
6. 1 Cor 15:24; Eph 1:21; 2:2; 3:10; 6:12; Col 1:16; 2:10, 15.
7. On these powers, see Dunn, *Theology of Paul*, 104–10.
8. 2 Cor 3:3; 6:16; 1 Thess 1:9; cf. 1 Tim 3:15; 4:10.

God is called living elsewhere in the Hebrew scriptures.[9] This is closely related to the presentation of God as the one, true God. By contrast with other so-called gods, who are not alive, God is living.

3. God Is Immortal, Eternal, Invisible

Paul occasionally refers to God as immortal (Rom 1:23; cf. 1 Tim 1:17; 6:16), eternal (Rom 16:26), or invisible (Col 1:15; cf. Rom 1:20; 1 Tim 1:17). These are not common descriptions of God in the Hebrew scriptures but derive from more abstract thought about God. These ideas are not greatly important for Paul, but he obviously thinks they are accurate.

4. God Possesses a Spirit

In Rom 8:9 Paul tells the Roman Christians,

The Spirit of God dwells in you.

Paul also refers to the Spirit of God in many other places,[10] and to the Spirit that comes from God (1 Cor 6:19) or the Spirit of the Lord (2 Cor 3:17). In Eph 4:30, 1 Thess 4:8, and 1 Cor 6:19, God's Spirit is called holy; very likely the Spirit of God is meant everywhere else Paul refers to the Holy Spirit.[11]

The basic meaning of the word "spirit" is "moving air." One of the most important instances of moving air is the breath that moves in and out of human beings and other living creatures. This breath can be seen as identical to their life. As long as they have breath, they have life. As we will see below in discussing Paul's anthropology, Paul sees human beings as spirit insofar as they are knowing, willing subjects.

God is said to have a Spirit by analogy with human beings. The Spirit of God is the life of God, God insofar as God knows and wills. (The wind is an instance of moving air that can be understood

---

9. See Deut 5:26; 2 Kgs 19:4, 16; Ps 84:3; Isa 37:4, 17.

10. Rom 8:11, 14; 15:19; 1 Cor 2:11, 14; 3:16; 6:11; 7:40; 12:3; 2 Cor 3:3; Eph 4:30; Phil 3:3; 1 Thess 4:8.

11. Rom 5:5; 9:1; 14:17; 15:13, 16; 1 Cor 12:3; 2 Cor 6:6; 13:13; Eph 1:13; 1 Thess 1:5, 6; cf 2 Tim 1:14; Titus 3:5; also "spirit of holiness" in Rom 1:4.

as symbolic of the Spirit of God.) Paul discusses the parallel between the Spirit of God and the human spirit in 1 Cor 2:10–12.

> For what human being knows what is truly human except the human spirit that is within? So also no one comprehends what is truly God's except the Spirit of God. (1 Cor 2:11)

Just as no one knows the things of the human being except the spirit of the human being within, so no one knows the things of God except the Spirit of God.

Paul derived the view that God possesses a Spirit, as well as his basic understanding of it, from the Hebrew scriptures.

5. God Is Glorious, Powerful, Wise, Righteous, Faithful, and True

Paul frequently refers to God as possessing a set of qualities that describe God's inherent virtue.

Paul sees God as glorious, that is, splendid, magnificent, like a source of light or one reflecting available light (cf. 1 Tim 6:16). In 2 Cor 4:6 Paul says,

> For it is the God who said, "Let light shine out of darkness," who has shone in our hearts to give the light of the knowledge of the glory of God in the face of Jesus Christ.

Paul also mentions the glory (δόξα) of God in other passages.[12]

God is also powerful and wise. Paul refers to the power of God in Rom 1:16 and other passages.[13] And Paul refers to the wisdom of God in Rom 11:33 and other passages.[14] He refers to God as wise in Rom 16:27; to wisdom from God in 1 Cor 1:30; and to what God knows in several passages.[15]

---

12. Rom 1:23; 3:23; 5:2; 15:7; 1 Cor 10:31; 11:7; 2 Cor 4:15; Eph 1:18; 3:16; Phil 1:11; 2:11; Col 1:11; 1 Thess 2:12; cf. 1 Tim 1:11; Titus 2:13. See also Paul's reference to God's riches in glory (Phil 4:19) and to God as Father of glory (Eph 1:17).

13. 1 Cor 1:18, 24; 2:5; 2 Cor 4:7; 6:7; 13:4 (twice); cf. 2 Tim 1:8. Paul speaks of being powerful in God in 2 Cor 10:4.

14. 1 Cor 1:21, 24; 2:7; Eph 3:10.

15. Rom 11:33; 2 Cor 11:11, 31; 12:2, 3.

Much of Paul's talk about the power and wisdom of God describes a distinctive understanding of these qualities in light of Christ. In 1 Cor 1:18–31 Paul says that Christ is the power of God and the wisdom of God (vv. 24, 30).

> 23 We proclaim Christ crucified, a stumbling block to Jews and foolishness to Gentiles, 24 but to those who are the called, both Jews and Greeks, Christ the power of God and the wisdom of God. (1 Cor 1:23–24)

Christ's crucifixion shows that God's power and wisdom are weak and foolish by ordinary human standards (v. 25), since Christ's crucifixion is foolishness by ordinary human standards (v. 18) and obviously manifests weakness. By acting through Christ, God destroyed the ordinary human understanding of wisdom (vv. 19–20), along with the ordinary human understanding of strength. God's power and wisdom are the true power and wisdom.[16]

In Rom 11:33–35 Paul describes the wisdom of God as unsearchable and inscrutable, supporting this with an appeal to Isa 40:13 and possibly Job 41:3.

> O the depth of the riches and wisdom and knowledge of God! How unsearchable are his judgments and how inscrutable his ways! (Rom 11:33)

In this case he is thinking of the way God used the unbelief of part of Israel to bring about the salvation of Gentiles and will eventually save all Israel (11:25–32).

God is also righteous, faithful, and true. The righteousness of God is God's justice, God's moral rectitude. Paul refers to the righteousness of God in Rom 1:17 and a number of other passages.[17] And Paul refers to the faithfulness of God in Rom 3:3 and to God

---

16. See H. Conzelmann, *Outline*, 241–44.

17. Rom 3:5, 21–22, 25–26; 10:3 (twice); 2 Cor 5:21; Phil 3:9. Paul refers to what is righteous with God in 2 Thess 1:6 and denies that God is unjust in Rom 3:5; 9:14. Moore says that justice and mercy are seen as the essential moral attributes of God in Judaism (*Judaism*, 1:386–96). On Paul's understanding of the righteousness of God, see Conzelmann, *Outline*, 214–20; Fitzmyer, "Pauline Teaching," 105–7.

as faithful in1 Cor 1:9 and other passages.[18] Paul refers to the truth of God in Rom 3:7 and 15:8, to God's being true in Rom 3:4, and to the sincerity of God in 2 Cor 1:12. Compare the reference to God as one who does not lie in Titus 1:2.

6. God Is Loving, Kind, Merciful, Compassionate, Consoling, the Source of Grace, Peace, and Hope

Paul very frequently refers to God as possessing a set of qualities that describe God as benevolent. This is the presentation of God that dominates Paul's references to God in himself.

Paul speaks of God's love for people in Rom 5:8.

> God proves his love for us in that while we still were sinners Christ died for us.

He also speaks of God's love for people in several other passages.[19] In Rom 1:7 Paul refers to those he addresses as God's beloved. Paul calls God the God of love in 2 Cor 13:11. He speaks of God as loving various people in Rom 8:37 and other passages.[20] He speaks of love as coming from God (Eph 6:23), of God as being for us (Rom 8:31), and of being approved by God (1 Thess 2:4). In 2 Cor 11:2 Paul speaks of God as having zeal for people.

Paul refers to the kindness (χρηστότης) of God in Rom 2:4 and other passages.[21] He speaks of the forbearance (ἀνοχή) of God in Rom 2:4 and 3:26 and the patience (μακροθυμία) of God in Rom 2:4 and 9:22.

---

18. 1 Cor 10:13; 2 Cor 1:18; 1 Thess 5:24. Paul refers to God as the God of steadfastness in Rom 15:5. In 2 Thess 3:3 Paul says that the Lord is faithful. In Rom 11:1–2 he says that God has not rejected his people Israel, alluding to Ps 94:14 (LXX 93:14).

19. Rom 5:5; 8:39; 2 Cor 13:13; 2 Thess 3:5. On the Jewish understanding of God as loving, see Moore, *Judaism*, 1:396–400.

20. Rom 9:13, 25; 2 Cor 9:7; Eph 2:4; 1 Thess 1:4; 2 Thess 2:13, 16.

21. Rom 11:22; Eph 2:7; cf. Titus 3:4.

Paul speaks of God as showing mercy in Rom 9:15 and a number of other passages.[22] He also refers to the mercy of God in Rom 15:9 and Eph 2:4.[23] Paul speaks of God's preparing vessels of mercy in Rom 9:23, and of the compassion of God in Rom 9:15; 12:1 and 2 Cor 1:3. He calls God the God of consolation in Rom 15:5 and 2 Cor 1:3. He speaks of being consoled by God in 2 Cor 1:4; 7:6. In Rom 14:3 Paul says that God has welcomed the weak.

The salutation of each of Paul's letters (except 1 Thessalonians) includes a wish that the recipients may have grace and peace from God.[24] For example, Rom 1:7 says,

> Grace to you and peace from God our Father and the Lord Jesus Christ.

Paul speaks of having peace with God in Rom 5:1 and says that God called Christians in peace in 1 Cor 7:15. He calls God the God of peace in Rom 15:33 and a number of other places.[25] Paul speaks of the peace of God in Phil 4:7.

Paul mentions the grace, or favor, of God in many places in addition to the salutations of his letters.[26] He also speaks of the grace given by God in Rom 15:15 and 2 Cor 9:14. Using the verb cognate to the noun "grace," Paul speaks of what God has bestowed, or will bestow, on people in Rom 8:32 and other passages.[27] Similarly, Paul speaks of the gift (χάρισμα) of God in Rom 6:23 and other places.[28] In Phil 4:19 Paul says that God will fulfill every need.

---

22. Rom 9:16, 18; 11:30–32; 2 Cor 4:1; Phil 2:27.

23. Cf. also 1 Tim 1:2; 2 Tim 1:2, 16 (mercy of the Lord), 18 (mercy of the Lord); Titus 3:5.

24. Rom 1:7; 1 Cor 1:3; 2 Cor 1:2; Gal 1:3; Eph 1:2; Phil 1:2; Col 1:2; 2 Thess 1:2; cf. 1 Tim 1:2; 2 Tim 1:2; Titus 1:4; Phlm 3. A similar wish is found in Eph 6:23–24. The salutation of 1 Thessalonians also includes the wish for grace and peace but does not explicitly say that this comes from God. The salutations of 1 and 2 Timothy add a wish for mercy to the wishes for grace and peace.

25. Rom 16:20; 1 Cor 14:33; 2 Cor 13:11; Phil 4:9; 1 Thess 5:23.

26. Rom 3:24; 5:15; 1 Cor 1:4; 3:10; 15:10 (three times); 2 Cor 1:12; 6:1; 8:1; 9:8, 14; 12:9; Gal 1:15; 2:21; Eph 1:6, 7; 2:7; 3:2, 7; Col 1:6; 2 Thess 1:12; 2:16; cf. Titus 2:11.

27. 1 Cor 2:14; Gal 3:18; Eph 4:32; Phil 1:29; 2:9.

28. Rom 11:29; 1 Cor 7:7; cf. 2 Tim 1:6. Paul also speaks of the gift (δῶρον) of God in Eph 2:8.

Finally Paul calls God the God of hope in Rom 15:13. Compare also the references to hope in God in 1 Tim 4:10; 5:5; 6:17.

7. The Wrath of God

Paul speaks of the wrath of God in several passages,[29] including Rom 1:18:

> The wrath of God is revealed from heaven against all ungodliness and wickedness of those who by their wickedness suppress the truth.

We should also probably understand Paul as speaking about the wrath of God in other places where he mentions wrath and does not explicitly say that it is God's.[30] Paul also refers to God as bringing down wrath (Rom 3:5) and showing wrath (Rom 9:22). He speaks of the severity of God (Rom 11:22) and of God as hating (Rom 9:13, quoting Mal 1:2–3).

The presentation of God as wrathful stands in some tension with the presentation of God as loving, and so forth. It flows naturally, however, from the presentation of God as righteous. God's righteousness issues in wrath against the unrighteous.

God in Relation to Others

Paul's letters refer to a number of ways God relates to others. We will discuss eight of them.

1. God Is Creator of All

Paul describes God as Creator when he says in Rom 4:17 that

> God…calls into existence the things that do not exist.

---

29. Rom 1:18; 13:4, 5; Eph 5:6; Col 3:6. On the wrath of God in Paul, see Conzelmann, *Outline*, 239–41.
30. Rom 2:5 (twice), 8; 4:15; 5:9; 12:19; Eph 2:3; 1 Thess 1:10; 2:16; 5:9.

Paul refers to the creation of the world in Rom 1:20. He implies that God is the Creator by saying that God's invisible power and divinity are seen in the things that were made. Paul refers to God as Creator more directly in Rom 1:25 and Eph 3:9; compare 1 Tim 4:3, 4. In several passages Paul describes God as Creator by quoting or alluding to the creation account in Genesis 1–2. In 2 Cor 4:6 Paul describes God as saying, "Let light shine out of darkness," paraphrasing Gen 1:3. In 1 Cor 11:7 Paul says that man is the image and glory of God, referring to Gen 1:27. In 1 Cor 11:8–9, 12 Paul speaks about woman's having come from man and having been created on account of man, referring to Gen 2:18–23. Paul also refers to God as Creator by saying that all things are from God and through God in Rom 11:36.

> For from him and through him and to him are all things. To him be the glory forever. Amen.

He also says that all things are from God in 1 Cor 8:6 and elsewhere.[31]

2. God Is Father

Paul calls God "Father" more often than he speaks about God as Creator; in part, calling God "Father" is another expression of the idea that God is Creator, using fatherhood as an image for creation. Paul speaks of God as Father in a number of places,[32] including 1 Cor 8:6.

> For us there is one God, the Father, from whom are all things and for whom we exist.

In various ways Paul refers to God specifically as the Father of Jesus; we will discuss this below in "The Person of Christ."

---

31. See 1 Cor 11:12; 2 Cor 5:18; cf. the statement that God gives life to all in 1 Tim 6:13. On the Jewish understanding of God as Creator, see Moore, *Judaism*, 1:380–85.
32. Rom 6:4; 1 Cor 8:6; 15:24; Gal 1:1, 3; Phil 2:11; 1 Thess 1:1; Eph 1:17; 2:18; 3:14–15; 5:20; 6:23; Col 1:12; 3:17; 2 Thess 1:2; cf. 1 Tim 1:2; 2 Tim 1:2; Titus 1:4.

Paul also frequently calls God the Father of people generally. In the salutations of all his letters (except the Pastoral Epistles), Paul refers to God as our Father[33] or our God and Father.[34] For example, 1 Cor 1:3 reads,

> Grace to you and peace from God our Father and the Lord Jesus Christ.

In Rom 8:15 and Gal 4:6 Paul says that Christians cry out to God, "Abba, Father." In 2 Cor 6:18 Paul presents God as saying, "I will be your father," paraphrasing 2 Sam 7:14. In Eph 4:6 Paul says that God is Father of all.

The idea that God is Father is also expressed by saying that people are children of God. Paul refers to Jews and Christians as sons of God in Rom 8:14 and elsewhere,[35] and as daughters of God in 2 Cor 6:18. He refers to them as children of God in Rom 8:16 and elsewhere,[36] and as seed of God in Rom 9:8. Paul speaks of Jews and Christians as receiving sonship of God in Rom 8:15 and elsewhere,[37] and of Jesus as the firstborn among many brothers in Rom 8:29.

God is often portrayed as Father in the Hebrew scriptures, postbiblical Jewish literature, and Greek literature.[38]

3. God Has a Will, a Law, a Plan, a Word

Paul refers to the will of God in Rom 1:10 and many other passages.[39] In the salutations of his letters he several times refers to himself as an apostle by the will of God.[40] For example, in 1 Cor 1:1 Paul identifies himself as

---

33. Rom 1:7; 1 Cor 1:3; 2 Cor 1:2; Eph 1:2; Phil 1:2; Col 1:2; 2 Thess 1:1; Phlm 3. This phrase is also found in 1 Thess 3:11 and 2 Thess 2:16.

34. Gal 1:4; 1 Thess 1:3. This phrase is also found in Phil 4:20 and 1 Thess 3:13.

35. Rom 8:19; 9:26 (quoting Hos 1:10 [LXX 2:1]); 2 Cor 6:18; Gal 3:26; 4:6–7.

36. Rom 8:17, 21; 9:8; Phil 2:15; Eph 5:1.

37. Rom 8:23; 9:4; Gal 4:5; Eph 1:5.

38. See Moore, *Judaism*, 2:201–11; G. Schrenk, G. Quell, "πατήρ κτλ.", *TDNT* 5:951–59, 965–74, 978–82; P. Gutierrez, *La paternité spirituelle selon Saint Paul*, 15–83; M. Hengel, *The Son of God*, 21–56.

39. Rom 2:18; 12:2; 15:32; 2 Cor 8:5; Gal 1:4; Eph 1:5, 9, 11; 6:6; Col 1:9; 4:12; 1 Thess 4:3; 5:18. He refers to the will of the Lord in Eph 5:17.

40. 1 Cor 1:1; 2 Cor 1:1; Eph 1:1; cf. 2 Tim 1:1.

Paul, called to be an apostle of Christ Jesus by the will of God.

Paul occasionally refers to the law of God, which presumably expresses God's will. We find such a reference in Rom 7:22.[41]

I delight in the law of God in my inmost self.

Paul also refers to the commandments of God (1 Cor 7:19), the command of God,[42] and the decree of God (Rom 1:32).[43] But Paul also refers to the law another 140 times (including 5 times in the Pastoral Epistles). Although he does not explicitly state that it is the law of God, this is clearly presupposed. Paul's extensive discussion of the law is not simply a presentation of it as the expression of God's will but is mainly an argument that Gentile Christians should not keep this law even though it expresses God's will.

Paul occasionally refers to the plan (πρόθεσις) of God. For instance, in Rom 8:28 Paul refers to those called according to God's plan.[44] He also speaks of the same reality in talking about the promises of God.[45] In the twenty-three other passages where Paul mentions promises without explicitly saying that they are God's promises (including twice in the Pastoral Epistles), this is clearly presumed. Paul also frequently refers to the word (λόγος) of God.[46] In Rom 9:6 Paul says that the word of God, that is, God's promise to save Israel, has not failed. Elsewhere Paul speaks of the content of his preaching as the word of God.[47] This is also an expression of

---

41. See also Rom 7:25; 8:7; cf. 1 Cor 9:21.

42. Rom 16:26; cf. 1 Tim 1:1; Titus 1:3.

43. In Rom 3:2 Paul says that the Jews were entrusted with the oracles of God. This would include the law of God as well as other parts of the Scriptures.

44. See also Rom 9:11; Eph 1:11; 3:11; cf. 2 Tim 1:9.

45. Rom 4:20; 2 Cor 1:20; Gal 3:21. Cf. the reference in Titus 1:2 to what God promised.

46. On the Jewish understanding of the word of God, see Moore, *Judaism*, 1:414–21.

47. 1 Cor 14:36; 2 Cor 2:17; 4:2; Phil 1:14; Col 1:25; 1 Thess 2:13 (twice); cf. 2 Tim 2:9; Titus 2:5. Paul uses ῥῆμα instead of λόγος in Eph 6:17 to express the same thing. In 1 Tim 4:5 the "word" of God may refer to prayer.

God's plan or promise of salvation. Similarly Paul refers to the content of his preaching as the gospel of God.[48]

4. God Reveals

Insofar as the law of God expresses God's will, it implies that God has revealed his will by giving the law. Likewise, to talk about the will of God in general or about the plan, promises, or word of God implies that somehow these have become known. The Hebrew scriptures explicitly present God as revealing the law through Moses and revealing promises and other words through the prophets. Paul also sometimes speaks more directly about God as revealer.

In Rom 1:19 Paul says that God has revealed (ἐφανέρωσεν) in creation what can be known about God. In Gal 1:16 he says that God revealed (ἀποκαλύψαι) his Son to Paul. He speaks of God's revelation to all Christians in 2 Cor 4:6 and Col 1:27. In 1 Cor 2:9–10 Paul says,

> 9 "What no eye has seen, nor ear heard, nor the human heart conceived, what God has prepared for those who love him"— 10 these things God has revealed to us through the Spirit.

In Phil 3:15 Paul says that God will reveal to those who think differently the truth of what Paul is saying.

5. God Is Sovereign

Twice Paul mentions God's foreknowledge (Rom 8:29; 11:2). This suggests the existence of a design in history that God accomplishes; it does not, however, necessarily imply this. It is more clearly indicated when Paul speaks about God as predestining, as he does in Rom 8:29 and elsewhere.[49] Paul expresses a more limited version of the same idea when he says that God set him apart from his mother's womb (Gal 1:15) or that God prepared something beforehand (Rom 9:23; Eph 2:10).

---

48. Rom 1:1; 15:16; 2 Cor 11:7; 1 Thess 2:2, 8, 9; cf. 1 Tim 1:11.
49. Rom 8:30; 1 Cor 2:7; Eph 1:5, 11.

Paul expresses the idea of God's sovereign control over human history in many other ways, particularly in Romans. In 1:24, 26, and 28 Paul says that God handed sinners over to various consequences of their sins. This at least means that God allowed the consequences of their choices to unfold and implies that God could have done otherwise. In Rom 8:32 Paul says that God handed Jesus over for all of us. Again this at least means that God could have done otherwise.

In Romans 9–11 Paul says that God has mercy on whomever God wishes and likewise hardens whomever God wishes.[50] Nevertheless, no human being can answer back to God; God is like a potter who can make whatever pots he wishes (9:20–21). In Rom 11:8 Paul explains how the hardening of part of Israel occurred by saying that God gave them a spirit of sluggishness, quoting Isa 29:10. Likewise, in Rom 11:32 Paul says that God imprisoned all in disobedience in order to be merciful to all (cf. 2 Thess 2:11). God has power to graft the branches removed from the cultivated olive tree, that is, Israel, back in again (Rom 11:23; cf. 2 Tim 2:25). Similarly Paul speaks about God's apportioning a measure of faith (Rom 12:3) and a situation in life (1 Cor 7:17) to each Christian, as well as a certain sphere of apostolic activity to Paul (2 Cor 10:13); compare also 2 Tim 1:7.

In Rom 13:1 Paul says that every authority comes from God and has been instituted by God. Therefore resistance to authority is resistance to what God has appointed (v. 2). The authority is the servant of God either for good or to execute wrath on those who do wrong (v. 4). Authorities are the ministers of God (v. 6).

Paul also presents God as sovereign by saying that God is responsible for various natural processes and for the realities of which these are images in Paul's discourse. Thus Paul says that God gives the growth of the fields in 1 Cor 3:6, 7; 2 Cor 9:10. In 1 Cor 15:38 Paul affirms that God gives the germinated seed a body. In 1 Cor 12:18 and 24 Paul says that God has arranged the human body as God chose; and in Col 2:19 he states that the growth of the body is God's work.

The view that God is sovereign is derived from the Hebrew scriptures.[51]

---

50. See Rom 9:15–18; 11:5–7.
51. See Moore, *Judaism*, 1:374–80.

6. God Calls, Saves, Makes Righteous, Reconciles; He Sent Jesus to Die and Raised Him from the Dead; He Sends the Spirit

Paul very frequently refers to God as possessing a set of qualities that describe God as Savior. This is the presentation of God that dominates Paul's references to God in relation to others.

Paul often says that God has called Jews and Christians. We find this in a number of passages,[52] including 1 Cor 1:9:

> God is faithful; by him you were called into the fellowship of his Son, Jesus Christ our Lord.

Paul also speaks of the call of God, saying in Rom 11:29 that the call of God is irrevocable.[53] And Paul refers to the people God has called as the elect of God.[54] In 1 Cor 8:3 and Gal 4:9 Paul says that God knows Christians.

Somewhat less often Paul says that God saved Christians; he does so in 1 Cor 1:21.[55] In Rom 1:16 Paul says that the gospel is the power of God for salvation; in Phil 1:28, that salvation is from God; and in 1 Thess 5:9 and 2 Thess 2:13, that God has destined Christians for salvation. In the Pastoral Epistles, God is called Savior.[56] Paul more often expresses the idea that God is Savior by saying that God makes Christians righteous. He mentions lack of righteousness with God as a problem in Rom 2:13. He says that God makes people righteous, or justifies them, in a number of passages,[57] including Rom 8:30:

---

52. Rom 8:30; 9:11, 24, 25; 1 Cor 1:9; 7:15, 17, 18–24; Gal 1:15; 1 Thess 2:12; 4:7; 5:24; 2 Thess 2:14; cf. 2 Tim 1:9. In a number of other passages, Paul does not make explicit who has called them, but it is likely Paul thinks that God has done so; Gal 5:8, 13; Eph 4:1, 4; cf. 1 Tim 6:12.

53. Other references to the call of God are found in Phil 3:14; 2 Thess 1:11; cf. 2 Tim 1:9.

54. Rom 8:33; Col 3:12; cf. Titus 1:1.

55. Cf. 2 Tim 1:9; Titus 3:5. 2 Tim 4:18 says that the Lord will save Paul.

56. 1 Tim 1:1; 2:3–4; 4:10; Titus 1:3; 2:10; 3:4.

57. Rom 3:24, 26, 30: 4:5; 5:1, 9; 8:30, 33; Gal 3:8.

Those whom he predestined he also called; and those whom he called he also justified; and those whom he justified he also glorified.

Paul also says that God reckons people righteous in Rom 4:6 and 24. Paul speaks of being made righteous before God in Gal 3:11 and of being made righteous by the Spirit of God in 1 Cor 6:11. Another of Paul's expressions of the saving activity of God is to say that God reconciles people to himself. We find references to alienation from God in Eph 2:12 and 4:18. Paul says that God reconciled people to himself in 2 Cor 5:18–19 (see also Col 1:20). Here Paul says that

God…reconciled us to himself through Christ. (2 Cor 5:18)

Paul refers to Christians as reconciled to God in Rom 5:10 and other passages.[58] In 1 Cor 15:57 Paul speaks of God as giving Christians victory.

God saved people by sending his Son Jesus (Rom 8:3; Gal 4:4), who belongs to God (1 Cor 3:23) and of whom God is head (1 Cor 11:3). God put Jesus forward as a sacrifice of atonement (Rom 3:25); in doing so, God did not spare his own Son (Rom 8:32).[59] God, who raises the dead (2 Cor 1:9), raised Jesus from the dead[60] and will raise Christians from the dead.[61] God exalted Jesus (Phil 2:9), who is now at the right hand of God.[62] The life of Christians is hidden with Christ in God (Col 3:3).

God sent Christians the Spirit of his Son (Gal 4:6). God sent the Spirit as a guarantee (2 Cor 1:21–22; 5:5). God is at work in the various manifestations of the Spirit given to the church (1 Cor 12:6, 28).

---

58. 2 Cor 5:20; Eph 2:16.

59. In Rom 11:21 Paul says that God did not spare the natural branches of the cultivated olive tree. Perhaps he sees some parallel between the death of Jesus and the unbelief of part of Israel, two elements of God's saving design.

60. See Rom 4:24, 25; 8:11 (twice); 10:9; 1 Cor 6:14; 15:15; 2 Cor 4:14; Gal 1:1; Eph 1:20; Col 2:12; 1 Thess 1:10.

61. See 1 Cor 6:14; 2 Cor 4:14; 5:5; 1 Thess 4:14.

62. See Rom 8:34; Eph 1:20; Col 3:1.

7. Christians Are the Congregation or Building of God

As a result of God's saving activity, Christians belong to God. Paul often refers to Christians as the congregation, or church, of God. We see this in many places,[63] including 1 Cor 1:2, where Paul addresses this letter to

the church of God that is in Corinth.

On a somewhat more intimate level, Paul speaks of Christians as members of God's household, or family, in Eph 2:19; compare 1 Tim 3:15. Still more intimately Paul describes Christians as having been made by God into a new man (Eph 4:24; Col 3:10). He also refers to Christians as the cultivated field of God in 1 Cor 3:9.

In 1 Cor 3:9 Paul also speaks of Christians as the building of God (cf. 2 Tim 2:19). He uses the metaphor of building to speak of his own apostolic activity in Rom 15:20 and 1 Cor 3:10–14, where he says,

According to the grace of God given to me, like a skilled master builder I laid a foundation. (1 Cor 3:10)

Paul also uses this metaphor to speak more generally about the effect of one's behavior on others.[64] Thus 1 Thess 5:11 says,

Therefore encourage one another and build up each other, as indeed you are doing.

Paul also speaks of Christians as the temple of God[65] or of the Holy Spirit (1 Cor 6:19). In 2 Cor 5:1 Paul says that Christians have a building from God.

---

63. 1 Cor 1:2; 10:32; 11:16, 22; 15:9; 2 Cor 1:1; Gal 1:13; 1 Thess 2:14; 2 Thess 1:4; cf. 1 Tim 3:5, 15. Paul speaks of the church in God in 1 Thess 1:1; 2 Thess 1:1.
64. See 1 Cor 8:1, 10; 10:23; 14:4 (twice), 17; 1 Thess 5:11.
65. See 1 Cor 3:16, 17; 2 Cor 6:16; Eph 2:21–22; Eph 2:22 also uses the phrase "dwelling place of God."

8. God Will Judge, Will Establish His Kingdom

Paul refers in various ways to his expectation that God will judge the world. He says precisely this in Rom 3:6. In Rom 2:5 he states that the just judgment of God will be revealed on the day of wrath, that is, at the end of the world.[66] Paul also says that the world will be held accountable to God (Rom 3:19) and that all must stand before the judgment seat of God (Rom 14:10), where each will give an account to God (v. 12). God will judge the hidden things of people (Rom 2:16; 1 Cor 4:5); at that time some will receive praise from God (1 Cor 4:5; cf. Rom 2:29). Paul also mentions the judgment of God in other passages.[67] He emphasizes that God does not show favoritism, that God is a just judge. Paul says this in Rom 2:11 and elsewhere.[68] It is a theme that derives from the Jewish understanding of God, as presented in 2 Chr 19:7 and elsewhere.

The result of God's judgment of the world is that the kingdom of God will be established. This is clearest in Paul's discussion of the events of the end time in 1 Corinthians 15. At the end Christ will hand over the kingdom to God (v. 24), and the living will be transformed (vv. 51–54) because flesh and blood cannot inherit the kingdom of God (v. 50). Paul also mentions the kingdom of God in Rom 14:17 and a number of other places.[69] When God's kingdom is established, God will be all in all (1 Cor 15:28).

Others in Relation to God

Paul's letters refer to a number of ways others should relate to God. We will discuss four of them.

---

66. There is another reference to the just judgment of God in 2 Thess 1:5. On Jewish expectations about the coming of the Messiah, the last judgment, and the establishment of the kingdom of God see Moore, *Judaism*, 2:323–76.

67. See Rom 2:2, 3; 11:33; 1 Cor 5:13.

68. Gal 2:6; Eph 6:9; Col 3:25. See J. Bassler, *Divine Impartiality*, who discusses the precedents for this theme in Jewish literature and its importance for Paul.

69. 1 Cor 4:20; 6:9, 10; Gal 5:21; Eph 5:5; Col 4:11; 1 Thess 2:12; 2 Thess 1:5; cf. reference to the Lord's kingdom in 2 Tim 4:18.

1. It Is Necessary to Know and Believe in God

In Rom 1:18–19 Paul refers to suppression of the truth, that is, what can be known about God, as deriving from unrighteousness. In Rom 1:28 he says that failing to hold God in recognition leads to unrighteousness. In Rom 3:11, quoting Ps 14:2 [LXX 13:2], Paul equates unrighteousness with failure to seek God. In 2 Cor 10:5 Paul says that he destroys every obstacle to knowledge of God. In Gal 4:8–9 he equates lack of knowledge of God with enslavement; in other places he sees other negative consequences of lack of knowledge of God.[70] In Col 1:10 Paul prays that the Colossians may grow in knowledge of God (see also Col 2:2).

It is also necessary to believe in God. Paul makes this point by presenting Abraham as a model because of his faith in God, indicated in Gen 15:6.[71] Paul also presents the Thessalonians' faith in God as a model for others in 1 Thess 1:8. In Rom 14:11 Paul quotes Isa 45:23 to say that every tongue must confess God.[72]

2. It Is Necessary to Love God, Give God Thanks, Honor, Glorify and Worship God, Pray to God, Boast in God

Paul speaks with approval of loving God in Rom 8:28 and 1 Cor 8:3; in 1 Cor 2:9 he does so by drawing upon a number of Old Testament passages. Similarly Paul speaks with approval about his own zeal for God (Gal 1:14; Phil 3:6) and that of the Jewish people in general (Rom 10:2). He sees this zeal, however, as partly misguided.

In Rom 1:21 Paul makes it clear that it is not enough to know God; one must also glorify God and give God thanks. Paul shows the latter by his example. Most of his letters begin with a prayer of thanksgiving to God.[73] For example, in Phil 1:3–4 he begins the thanksgiving prayer this way:

---

70. See Rom 10:2; 1 Cor 15:34; 1 Thess 4:5; 2 Thess 1:8.

71. See Rom 4:3, 5, 17, 24; Gal 3:6.

72. There is another reference to belief in God in Titus 3:8.

73. See Rom 1:8; 1 Cor 1:4; Phil 1:3; Col 1:3; 1 Thess 1:2; 2 Thess 1:3; Phlm 4; cf. 2 Tim 1:3.

> I thank my God every time I remember you, constantly pray-
> ing with joy in every one of my prayers for all of you.

He also expresses thanks to God at other points in his letters,[74] often using the formula "thanks be to God."[75] Paul also frequently speaks about Christians in general giving thanks to God.[76] He shows the need to glorify God by saying that Abraham did so (Rom 4:20) and by glorifying God in doxologies.[77] For example, in Gal 1:4–5 Paul praises God thus:

> Our God and Father, to whom be the glory forever and ever.
> Amen.

Paul speaks about the desirability that Christians glorify God in Rom 15:6 and other passages.[78] He says that Christians do glorify God in Gal 1:24. Similarly, Paul is critical of dishonoring God (Rom 2:23), of having the name of God blasphemed (Rom 2:24, quoting Isa 52:5), and of mocking God (Gal 6:7).[79] Paul urges the Thessalonians to be worthy of God in 1 Thess 2:12.

In various ways Paul presupposes that people should worship God. He says that the person who detects the presence of God among Christians will bow down and worship God (1 Cor 14:25). Paul also uses the worship of offering sacrifice as a metaphor for various aspects of Christian living. This presumes that such wor-ship is good but also that it will not be carried out literally. In Rom 12:1 Paul tells the Roman Christians to present themselves as a liv-ing sacrifice to God. In 2 Cor 2:15 he says that he and others are "the aroma of Christ to God," perhaps envisioning himself as the

---

74. See 1 Cor 1:14; 14:18; Eph 1:16; 1 Thess 2:13; 3:9; 2 Thess 2:13.

75. See Rom 6:17; 7:25; 1 Cor 15:57; 2 Cor 2:14; 8:16; 9:15.

76. See Rom 14:6 (twice); 2 Cor 9:12; Eph 5:20; Col 1:12; 3:17.

77. See Rom 11:36; 16:27; Gal 1:5; Eph 3:21; Phil 4:20; cf. 1 Tim 1:17. 2 Tim 4:18 is a doxology to the Lord.

78. See Rom 15:9; 1 Cor 6:20; 2 Cor 1:20; 9:13; Phil 1:11; 2 Thess 3:1. In Eph 1:6, 12, and 14 Paul speaks of praising the glory of God. In 2 Cor 8:19 Paul describes as desirable acting for the glory of the Lord.

79. Note in 1 Tim 6:1 the criticism of having the name of God blasphemed and in Titus 2:5 that of having the word of God blasphemed. Honor is given to God in 1 Tim 1:17; 6:16.

smoke of a sacrifice offered to God. In Phil 2:17 Paul says that he is poured out as a libation over the sacrifice and offering of the Philippians' faith (cf. 2 Tim 4:6). In Phil 4:18 he says that the Philippians' gift to him was "a fragrant offering, a sacrifice acceptable and pleasing to God."

Paul shows that prayer to God is good by frequently praying in his letters. He does so in the thanksgiving prayers and doxologies mentioned above. In addition, Paul prays a blessing prayer instead of a thanksgiving prayer at the beginning of two letters (2 Cor 1:3; Eph 1:3). In 2 Corinthians this blessing prayer begins,

> Blessed be the God and Father of our Lord Jesus Christ, the Father of mercies and the God of all consolation.

Paul also prays at other points in his letters. He prays for the Jewish people (Rom 9:3; 10:1) and for the recipients of many of his letters.[80] Paul asks the recipients of his letters to pray in Rom 12:12 and other passages.[81] Paul often takes it for granted that Christians pray. This is the case in 1 Cor 11:2–16, where Paul discusses women and men's dress while they pray (vv. 4–5, 13). Likewise in 1 Cor 14:2 and 28 Paul says that speaking in tongues is speaking to God; in verses 14–15 he says that speaking in tongues is prayer in the Spirit.[82] In Rom 8:26–27 Paul says that the Spirit helps Christians to pray because they do not know how to pray as they ought.

Paul says that Jews and Christians must boast in God. In Rom 2:17 he describes Jews as ones who boast in God. In Rom 5:2 and 11 he says that Christians boast in God. In Rom 4:2 Paul states that Abraham could not boast of his accomplishments before God; in 1 Cor 1:29 he says that no one can boast before God. Instead one who boasts should boast in the Lord (1 Cor 1:31; 2 Cor 10:17,

---

80. See 2 Cor 13:7, 9; Phil 1:9; Eph 3:14–19; Col 1:9; 2 Thess 1:11. On prayer in Judaism, see Moore, *Judaism*, 2:212–36.

81. See Rom 15:30; 1 Cor 7:5; 14:13; Eph 6:18–20; Phil 4:6; Col 4:2–3; 1 Thess 5:17, 25; 2 Thess 3:1. In Col 3:16 Paul tells the Colossians to sing prayers to God. 1 Tim 2:1 and 8 also direct Christians to pray.

82. Paul also refers to the prayer of Christians in 2 Cor 1:11; 9:14; Phil 1:19; Col 4:12; Phlm 22; cf. 1 Tim 5:5.

quoting Jer 9:22–23). In Rom 15:17, however, Paul says that he can boast of his work for God.

3. It Is Necessary to Fear, Please, and Serve God

Paul occasionally refers to the necessity of fearing God. In Rom 3:18 he quotes Ps 36:2 (LXX 35:2) as saying that the unrighteous do not have fear of God. In 2 Cor 5:11 and 7:1 he speaks of himself and others as having fear of God.

More frequently Paul speaks of needing to please God. He indicates this indirectly by saying that those in the flesh cannot please God (Rom 8:8) and that those who oppose the Christian mission displease God (1 Thess 2:15). He urges people to please God in Rom 12:1–2 and other passages.[83] Paul implies that he seeks approval from God in Gal 1:10, and describes the Philippians' gift to him as pleasing to God (Phil 4:18). He says that God was not pleased with the wilderness generation in 1 Cor 10:5 and that God was pleased to do things in 1 Cor 1:21 and Gal 1:15.

Paul speaks of Christians' serving God as slaves (δουλεύειν) in Rom 6:22 and 1 Thess 1:9; compare Titus 1:1. He speaks of being a servant (διάκονος) of God in Rom 13:4 and 2 Cor 6:4.[84] Paul mentions obeying God in Rom 11:30 and not rejecting God in 1 Thess 4:8. He urges people to present their members to God as weapons of righteousness in Rom 6:13 (cf. 2 Tim 2:15). Paul speaks of bearing fruit to God in Rom 7:4.

4. Christians Live in the Presence of God, Live to God, Belong to God; God Works in and through Them

Paul refers to Christians as being before (ἐνώπιον) God in Rom 3:20 and other passages.[85] He also speaks of himself and oth-

---

83. Rom 14:18; 1 Thess 4:1. In Eph 5:10 he urges them to please the Lord.

84. Titus 1:7 speaks of being a steward (οἰκονόμος) of God.

85. Rom 14:22; 1 Cor 1:29; 2 Cor 4:2; 7:12; Gal 1:20; cf. 1 Tim 2:3; 5:4, 21; 6:13; 2 Tim 2:14; 4:1. He expresses the same idea, using the word ἔμπροσθεν, in 1 Thess 1:3; 3:9, 13.

ers as being in the sight of (κατέναντι) God in 2 Cor 2:17 and 12:19.

Paul says that Christians live to God in Rom 6:10–11 and Gal 2:19 and urges them to do so in Rom 6:13. In 1 Cor 8:6 he refers to God as the one for whom we exist. In 2 Cor 6:16 he quotes Ezek 37:27, in which God says, "I will be their God, and they will be my people." Paul refers to God as "my God" in Rom 1:8 and elsewhere.[86] Likewise Paul refers to God as his witness in Rom 1:9 and elsewhere.[87]

In 1 Cor 14:25 Paul says that God is among Christians; in Phil 2:13, that God is at work in Christians; and in 2 Cor 2:17, that he and others are from God. Paul describes himself and others as coworkers of God in 1 Cor 3:9 and 1 Thess 3:2.[88] He describes himself as a witness of God in 1 Cor 15:15.

Summary Observations

In general, Paul's understanding of God is the Jewish understanding of God.[89] We have noted above many points at which Paul speaks of God by quoting, or alluding to, Old Testament passages. We have noted specifically that Paul's presentation of God as one and living, as possessing a Spirit, as righteous, loving, and merciful, as Creator of all, as Father, as speaking a word, as revealer, as sovereign, and as a just judge derive from the Jewish understanding of God. We have also noted that Paul's view that one should pray to God derives from Judaism.

Some elements of Paul's picture of God derive specifically from Jewish apocalyptic thinking. The biblical ideas that God has a plan, reveals that plan, is sovereign, and would send a savior, judge the world, and establish the kingdom of God were emphasized and took on new meaning in the context of apocalyptic thinking. The idea that God would raise the dead seems to have been unique to apocalyptic thought.

---

86. See Phil 1:3; 4:19; Phlm 4.
87. See 2 Cor 1:23; Phil 1:8; 1 Thess 2:5, 10.
88. Cf. also references to the man of God in 1 Tim 6:11; 2 Tim 3:17.
89. See Dunn, *Theology of Paul*, 29–31.

Paul's presentation of God as immortal, eternal, and invisible seems to derive from Greek thought about God, probably as mediated by Hellenistic Jews such as Philo of Alexandria. Paul's presentation of God as one and as Father has parallels in Greek thought about God as well as in Judaism. His way of speaking about the oneness of God has probably been influenced by Stoic formulations mediated to Paul by Hellenistic Judaism.[90]

Finally, at a number of points, Paul's picture of God has been influenced by his faith in Jesus. We have noted the way Paul's understanding of God as one is qualified by setting the one Lord Jesus Christ alongside God. We have also noted the distinctive understanding of God's power and wisdom that derives from belief that God acted through the crucifixion of Jesus. In presenting God as Father, Paul sees him specifically as the Father of Jesus. Because of his faith in Jesus, Paul argues that Gentile Christians should not keep God's law. Most important of all, Paul sees God as having saved Christians by sending his Son Jesus.

---

90. See M. Dibelius, "Die Christianisierung einer hellenistischen Formel"; E. Norden, *Agnostos Theos*, 240–50.

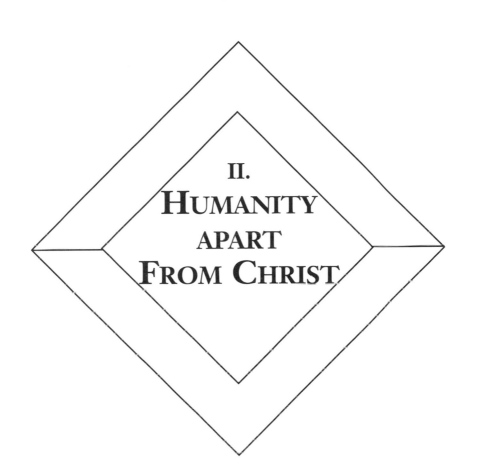

II.
HUMANITY
APART
FROM CHRIST

In order to grasp Paul's understanding of the significance of Christ, it is necessary first to understand the problem for which Christ is the solution. We must begin by analyzing the need for salvation; then we can understand how Christ answers this need. Paul himself sums up the plight of the human race apart from Christ in Rom 3:23:

All have sinned and fall short of the glory of God.

In a word, sin is the reason the human race needs salvation. This is a familiar analysis of the human situation apart from Christ. We must be wary, however, of presuming too easily that what Paul means by sin is identical to our understanding. As we will see, the two differ significantly.

Plight and Solution

Logically, plight precedes solution. But this does not necessarily mean that understanding of plight precedes acceptance of solution in any individual's experience. It is possible that someone first accept Christ as the Savior of the human race and work back from this acceptance to the understanding of the human plight that is implied by it. In this case, acceptance of Christ as Savior would be based primarily on something other than the perception of him as the solution to the human plight. Such a perception, however, would need to follow upon this acceptance in order to make sense of it.

E. P. Sanders has proposed, correctly in my judgment, that for Paul acceptance of Christ as solution preceded Paul's analysis of the human plight.[1] His acceptance of Jesus as Christ, that is, Savior, was based on his encounter with the risen Jesus. Paul then had to work

---

1. E. P. Sanders, *Paul and Palestinian Judaism*, 442–47. Cf. also G. Bornkamm, *Paul*, 120–22.

out an understanding of the human plight with this as his starting point. F. Thielman, however, has argued that Sanders is wrong.[2]

This question is interesting in itself but makes little difference for our synthesis of Paul's theology. The way Paul arrived at his understanding of the human situation apart from Christ does not affect its place in his theology. The main importance of the question lies in its implications for Paul's view of Judaism. If Paul's awareness of the human plight preceded his conversion, he began with a negative view of Judaism. He was dissatisfied with it because it did not solve the basic problem of the human race, that is, sin. On the other hand, if his conversion preceded his analysis of the human plight, he need not have had a negative view of Judaism. He might have been entirely satisfied as a Jew until his conversion made him see that Judaism had not solved the problem of sin.

Anthropology

Paul's understanding of sin is based on his understanding of human nature. Paul never addresses this topic itself, but his understanding of human nature is indicated by his use of certain terms that imply it. He uses some of the same terms we use to speak of human nature, but a close examination shows that he means something different by them than we usually do. Thus they imply a different anthropology for Paul than they do for us.

1. Differences between Paul's Anthropology and Ours

"Body" (σῶμα) and "soul" (ψυχή) are two central anthropological terms we share with Paul. For us, these terms tend to denote two components of the human being. *Webster's New Collegiate Dictionary* defines body as "the organized physical substance of an animal or plant either living or dead," and soul as "the immaterial essence, animating principle, or actuating cause of an individual life." Thus the body is the physical, material component of an animal or plant, and the soul is the immaterial, actuating component

2. F. Thielman, *From Plight to Solution*.

of the animal or plant. In addition, Christians and others regard the human soul as intrinsically immortal. It separates from the body at death but is not itself harmed by death. Thus body and soul are two parts of the human being that are essentially different from one another.

Plato gave classical expression to this understanding of human nature in the fourth century BCE (e.g., in *Phaedo*). In the centuries after Plato, some philosophers moved away from the understanding of the soul as immortal, and many followed their views. Others continued to maintain a view like Plato's. For example, the Nemrud Dagh inscription, dating from the middle of the first century BCE, speaks about a resting place for the body of the king's form, his soul having been dispatched to the heavenly thrones of the gods. Jews who were especially influenced by Platonic philosophy adopted a view like this. For example, Philo of Alexandria refers to

> the unstable things of chance, none of which has anything to do with our noblest part, the soul or mind, but all are related to that dead thing which was our birth-fellow, the body.
>
> (*Gigantibus* 15)

Likewise, the biblical book of Wisdom says,

> For a perishable body weighs down the soul, and this earthly tent burdens the thoughtful mind. (9:15; cf. 3:1)

And this understanding is presumed by Christians today.

For Paul, however, body and soul are not two separable components of the human being; rather they are two aspects of the human being. Each refers to the whole human being but seen from a particular perspective.

Such a view is similar to Aristotle's understanding of body and soul. For Aristotle, "body" is the matter, and "soul" the form of the human being. Without both matter and form, there is no human being. It is not likely that Paul's view derived in any measure from Aristotle. Rather it is more likely to come from a strand of Jewish thought that was little influenced by Greek philosophy, namely, apocalyptic expectation. Apocalyptic expectation awaits life after death in the form of resurrection from the dead. This implies that a human being must be both body and soul in order to exist at all. Paul awaits resurrection from the dead and accepts this implication.

Although Paul's anthropology probably derives from Jewish apocalyptic thinking, it is not expressed in terms that come directly from Hebrew literature. There is no real Hebrew equivalent to the Greek word for "body" or for "mind," another important term for Paul that we will discuss below, but the meaning of these words for Paul is not simply their ordinary meaning in Greek. There is a Hebrew equivalent to the Greek word for "soul" as also for "spirit," "heart," and "flesh," other terms we will discuss below, but again the meaning of these words for Paul is not simply their ordinary meaning in Hebrew or Greek.[3] Paul expresses his anthropology in new language, making it easy to misunderstand his meaning if we are not careful.

Christians today affirm both the immortality of the soul and the hope for resurrection. The former is sure to be expressed at any funeral; the latter is part of the Nicene Creed. There is some tension between these affirmations. If the soul is immortal and can be with God immediately after death, what is the purpose of resurrection? Why reunite body and soul? There seems little need for it. It is my impression that immortality of the soul dominates the thinking of the ordinary Christian today whereas hope for resurrection receives little attention. This minimizes awareness of the tension between them.

2. Paul's Anthropology

a) Body

If Paul uses "body" and "soul" to indicate two aspects of the human being, it remains to say what these two aspects are. Rudolf Bultmann argues that, for Paul, "body" means the human being

> in respect to his being able to make himself the object of his own action or to experience himself as the subject to whom something happens.[4]

---

3. See Dunn, *Theology of Paul*, 54.

4. R. Bultmann, *Theology of the New Testament*, 1:195. Bultmann discusses the meaning of "body" in the letters of Paul on pp. 192–203. On this topic, see

42

Thus, "body" denotes the human being as recipient of action, either one's own action or that of someone or something else. Paul uses the word "body" very frequently and not always with this meaning.[5] But this is its core meaning for Paul.

This meaning is particularly clear in Romans 6:12–13, where

> do not let sin exercise dominion in your mortal bodies

is parallel to

> present yourselves to God.

"Your bodies" has the same meaning as "yourselves," that is, the person as the recipient of his or her own action, either of allowing sin to exercise dominion or of presenting oneself to God. Likewise,

> your bodies are members of Christ (1 Cor 6:15)

is parallel to

> you are the body of Christ and individually members of it.
> (1 Cor 12:27)

"Your bodies" has the same meaning as "you," that is, the person as recipient of the action of having been made part of the body of Christ.

b) "Soul" and Other Terms

"Soul," on the other hand, is one of a series of terms Paul uses to mean the human being as "the subject of his own willing and doing."[6] This meaning is clear in Phil 1:27, where Paul urges his readers to strive

---

Robinson, *The Body*, 26–33; Bornkamm, *Paul*, 130–31; H. Ridderbos, *Paul*, 115–17; Conzelmann, *Outline*, 176–78; J. C. Beker, *Paul the Apostle*, 287–91; Dunn, *Theology of Paul*, 55–61.

5. σῶμα occurs seventy-eight times in the letters of Paul, including nine times in Ephesians and eight times in Colossians.

6. Bultmann, *Theology of the New Testament*, 1:203. Bultmann discusses the meaning of "soul" in the letters of Paul on pp. 203–5. See also Conzelmann, *Outline*, 179. Bornkamm (*Paul*, 131–32) briefly discusses "soul" and related terms.

side by side with one soul for the faith of the gospel.

We can also see it in Rom 2:9, where Paul refers to

every soul of a human being doing evil,

and 13:1, where Paul says,

Let every soul be subject to the governing authorities.

Paul uses the word "soul" rather infrequently and not always clearly with this meaning.[7] Paul also uses a number of other terms, however, to indicate the human being as the knowing, willing subject.

One of these is "spirit" (πνεῦμα). Most often Paul uses this term to designate the Spirit of God.[8] But at times he uses it to refer to the human spirit, and then it has the meaning mentioned above. One instance of this is Phil 1:27, where

standing firm in one spirit

is parallel to

striving side by side with one soul.

Another instance is Rom 1:9, where Paul refers to serving God in his (Paul's) spirit.[9]

Other terms Paul uses to denote the human being as the knowing, willing subject are "mind" (νοῦς) and "heart" (καρδία).

---

7. ψυχή occurs thirteen times in the letters of Paul, including once in Ephesians and once in Colossians.

8. Dunn estimates that well over 100 of the 146 occurrences of πνεῦμα in the letters of Paul refer to the Spirit of God (*Theology of Paul*, 76 n 117).

9. I count nineteen other passages in which πνεῦμα refers to the human spirit—Rom 12:11; 1 Cor 2:11; 4:21; 5:3, 4, 5; 7:34; 16:18; 2 Cor 2:13; 4:13; 7:1, 13; 12:18; Gal 6:1; Eph 4:23; Col 2:5; 1 Thess 5:23; 2 Tim 4:22; Phlm 25. On "spirit" in the letters of Paul, see Bultmann, *Theology of the New Testament*, 1.205–9; Conzelmann, *Outline*, 180. Ridderbos (*Paul*, 120–21) and Dunn (*Theology of Paul*, 76–78) discuss "soul" and "spirit" together.

We see this use of "mind" in 1 Cor 1:10, where Paul urges the Corinthians to

> be united in the same mind and the same purpose.

Likewise, in Rom 12:2 Paul exhorts the Romans to

> be transformed by the renewing of your minds.[10]

The use of "heart" in the same sense can be seen in 2 Cor 3:14–15.

> A veil lies over their heart (v. 15)

parallels

> their minds [νοήματα] were hardened. (v. 14)

In 1 Cor 7:37 Paul refers to the possibility that someone stand "firm in his heart." "Heart" is the term Paul uses most frequently to denote the human being as the knowing, willing subject.[11]

c) Paul's Basic Conception of the Human Being

Analysis of Paul's use of the terms "body," on the one hand, and "soul," "spirit," "mind," and "heart," on the other, shows that, for Paul, the two fundamental aspects of the human being are the abilities to act and to be acted upon. These are combined in the ability to act upon oneself. From the time of Plato to the present, many have regarded the human being as basically an immortal, immaterial soul united to a mortal, physical body. By contrast, Paul

---

10. νοῦς occurs a total of twenty-one times in the letters of Paul, including twice in Ephesians and once each in Colossians, 2 Thessalonians, 1 Timothy, 2 Timothy, and Titus. On "mind" in the letters of Paul, see Bultmann, *Theology of the New Testament*, 1:211–20; Ridderbos, *Paul*, 117–19; Conzelmann, *Outline*, 180–81.

11. καρδία occurs fifty-two times in the letters of Paul, including six times in Ephesians, five in Colossians, twice in 2 Thessalonians, and once each in 1 Timothy and 2 Timothy. On "heart" in the letters of Paul, see Bultmann, *Theology of the New Testament*, 1:220–27; Ridderbos, *Paul*, 119–20; Conzelmann, *Outline*, 183–84. Dunn discusses "mind" and "heart" together (*Theology of Paul*, 73–75).

sees the human being basically as a unity that can both act and be acted upon and can act upon itself.

For Paul, being human fundamentally means that one can be under either one's own control or the control of another. And being under the control of another can be either control by a hostile power that sets the human being in opposition to himself or herself or control by a friendly power that maintains or restores the harmony of the human being with himself or herself. In the words of Bultmann:

> The possibility of having one's self in hand or of losing this control and being at the mercy of a power not one's own is inherent to human existence itself. But in the latter situation the outside power can be experienced as an enemy power which estranges man from himself or as the opposite, a friendly power that brings the man estranged from himself back to himself.[12]

For Paul, sin means losing control of oneself to a hostile power that sets the human being in opposition to himself or herself. It also means being in the state of having lost control to such a hostile power. Paul often uses the word "flesh" (σάρξ) to mean being in this state.[13] As we will see, salvation means coming under the control of a friendly power that restores the harmony of the human being with himself or herself. And salvation not only restores the harmony that was lost but also allows resumption of development toward the ultimate union with God for which human beings were created.

d) Flesh

The word "flesh," in both Greek and English, literally means the soft tissues of an animal body. Paul sometimes uses the word with this meaning—for example, when he uses "flesh and blood" in

---

12. Bultmann, *Theology of the New Testament*, 1:196.

13. σάρξ occurs ninety-one times in the letters of Paul, including nine times in Ephesians, nine times in Colossians, and once in 1 Timothy. On "flesh" in the letters of Paul, see Bultmann, *Theology of the New Testament*, 1:232–46; Robinson, *The Body*, 17–26; Bornkamm, *Paul*, 133; Ridderbos, *Paul*, 93–95; Conzelmann, *Outline*, 178–79; Dunn, *Theology of Paul*, 62–70.

1 Cor 15:50; Gal 1:16 to designate human beings. But Paul most characteristically uses "flesh" in a nonliteral sense to mean being in the state of sin.

Use of "flesh" in this sense can be seen in Rom 7:5, where Paul says,

> While we were living in the flesh, our sinful passions, aroused by the law, were at work in our members to bear fruit for death.

Paul refers to living in the flesh as something in the past for himself and those he addresses. This makes it clear that he uses the term in a nonliteral sense because they continue to be in the flesh in a literal sense. What Paul means by "flesh" here is being in the state where sinful passions are at work in people to bear fruit for death.

This same use of "flesh" can be seen in Rom 8:3–9. In verse 4 Paul describes himself and those he addresses as ones

> who walk not according to the flesh but according to the Spirit.

This contrast indicates that walking according to the flesh means being guided by something contrary to the Spirit of God. That this is sin rather than flesh in the literal sense is clear from verses 8–9, where Paul says that

> those who are in the flesh cannot please God. But you are not in the flesh.

We have earlier discussed the differences between what Paul means by "body" and "soul" and what we spontaneously take them to mean. Because of this we can easily misunderstand what Paul says about body and soul. We can even more easily misunderstand Paul's use of "flesh" and take it literally. This is true both because Paul sometimes uses the word literally and because we use it literally ourselves. To take Paul's use of "flesh" literally has the effect of making Paul seem to be very negative toward embodied existence. But as we have seen above, not only was he not negative toward embodied existence; he envisioned no other kind of human existence.

Sin

Our examination of Paul's anthropology has shown that, for Paul, sin means essentially losing control of oneself to a hostile power that sets the human being in opposition to himself or herself. It remains to explore Paul's understanding of sin in more detail.[14] Paul himself discusses this topic at some length in Rom 1:18—3:20; we will discuss this passage below. Here we will set out Paul's understanding of sin schematically.

1. Sin Is Idolatry

For Paul, sin is most basically idolatry, offering to something other than God the glory and thanks that are due to God.[15] Because God is the Creator of human beings and the world in which they live, the proper way for human beings to exercise control over themselves is to submit to the control of God. Accepting the control of God means accepting the reality of being God's creature. Thus, yielding control of oneself to God means being controlled by a friendly power that maintains the harmony of the human being with himself or herself.

Not yielding control of oneself to God means putting something else in the place of God, which by definition is a false god. This can take the form of recognizing some power other than God as god or of trying to be one's own god. In either case the person who does this yields control of himself or herself to someone other than God and bases his or her existence on a lie.

Paul probably derived these views from reading Genesis 3. According to this passage, the serpent tempted the first woman to eat the fruit of the tree in the middle of the garden by telling her,

---

14. On sin in Paul's thought, see Conzelmann, *Outline*, 192–98.

15. On sin as idolatry, see Bultmann, *Theology of the New Testament*, 1:228–29, 232, 239; Ridderbos, *Paul*, 105–6.

when you eat of it your eyes will be opened and you will be like
God, knowing good and evil. (Gen 3:5)

The woman ate the fruit in order to be her own god, rejecting sub-
mission to God. In doing so, she made a god of her own belly (cf.
Phil 3:19), putting it before God's directive. Shortly afterward the
first man did the same. All human ill resulted from this choice.

After Romans 1, which we will discuss below, Paul's most
extensive discussion of sin as idolatry is found in 1 Cor 10:1–13.
Paul's point in this passage is stated in 1 Cor 10:14, "flee from the
worship of idols." Wayne Meeks has argued that verses 1–13 are a
homily on Exod 32:6, which is quoted in verse 7, "The people sat
down to eat and drink and rose up to play."[16] This verse is part of
the account of Israel's idolatrous worship of the golden calf after
the exodus from Egypt (Exodus 32–34). According to Meeks,
verses 1–4, which recite a list of God's gracious acts for Israel, elaborate the first part of the verse, "The people sat down to eat and
drink."

> 1 I do not want you to be unaware, brothers and sisters, that
> our ancestors were all under the cloud, and all passed through
> the sea, 2 and all were baptized into Moses in the cloud and in
> the sea, 3 and all ate the same spiritual food, 4 and all drank the
> same spiritual drink. For they drank from the spiritual rock
> that followed them, and the rock was Christ.

Verses 6–10, which list Israel's sins despite that grace, elaborate the
second part of the verse, "and rose up to play."

> 6 Now these things occurred as examples for us, so that we
> might not desire evil as they did. 7 Do not become idolaters
> as some of them did; as it is written, "The people sat down to
> eat and drink, and they rose up to play." 8 We must not indulge
> in sexual immorality as some of them did, and twenty-three
> thousand fell in a single day. 9 We must not put Christ to the
> test, as some of them did, and were destroyed by serpents.

---

16. Meeks, "'And Rose Up to Play,'" 66. See also T. Callan, "Paul and the Golden
Calf."

10 And do not complain as some of them did, and were destroyed by the destroyer.

Meeks shows that the word "play" (παίζειν/צחק) is used in Jewish interpretation to designate all of the sins mentioned in these verses, that is, desiring evil things, idolatry, sexual immorality, putting God to the test, and complaining. This way of relating Israel's sins in general to its worship of the golden calf seems to imply that idolatry is the root of all sin.

2. Sin Is Slavery

Because idolatry is yielding control of oneself to a hostile power, the understanding of sin as slavery follows directly from understanding sin as idolatry.[17] As Paul sees it, when human beings choose to submit themselves to something other than God, they lose their freedom to make a different choice. They become the slaves of this false god, forced to do its bidding whether willingly or not.

Human beings seek life. All life comes from God; therefore, life can be found only in acceptance of the truth that God is Creator and humans are creatures of God. When humans try to be self-sufficient or seek life in something other than God, they turn away from the only source of life and find death instead of life. Death is the result of idolatry and the clearest sign that idolatry leads to slavery. Having submitted to something other than God, human beings must suffer death, whether they want to or not. We tend to see death as something natural, simply part of the world as we know it. For Paul, death is unnatural, not intended by God to occur at all. Death is a result of sin. If there had been no sin, there would be no death.

Paul probably derived this view from Genesis 2–3. According to Genesis, God forbade the first human being to eat the fruit of the tree of knowledge of good and evil, warning that if the human being did so, he would die (Gen 2:17; 3:3). After the first man and woman did eat the fruit, God said to the man, "You

---

17. On sin as slavery, see Bultmann, *Theology of the New Testament*, 1:243–49. Ridderbos sees slavery and death as punishments for sin (*Paul*, 112–14).

are dust and to dust you shall return" (Gen 3:19). Then the man and the woman were driven out of the garden of Eden (Gen 3:24) and deprived of access to the tree of life (see Gen 2:9).

Paul's view that death is a result of sin may imply that human sinfulness brought death not only to humans but also to all other living things. Thus, at least in this way, human sinfulness affected the entire world. This is probably what Paul means when he says in Rom 8:20–21 that creation was subjected to futility and is now in bondage to corruption. Paul may see the cosmic consequences of sin indicated in Genesis 3, where childbirth is made painful (v. 16) and the ground cursed (vv. 17–19a) because of Adam and Eve's sin.

Paul refers to the slavery of human beings apart from Christ in Gal 4:1–11.

> 1 My point is this: heirs, as long as they are minors, are no better than slaves, though they are the owners of all the property; 2 but they remain under guardians and trustees until the date set by the father. 3 So with us; while we were minors, we were enslaved to the elemental spirits of the world....7 So you are no longer a slave but a child, and if a child then also an heir, through God. 8 Formerly, when you did not know God, you were enslaved to beings that by nature are not gods. 9 Now, however, that you have come to know God, or rather to be known by God, how can you turn back again to the weak and beggarly elemental spirits? How can you want to be enslaved to them again?

Here Paul compares the situation of the heir, while a minor, to that of a slave (v. 1). He explains that Jews ("we") were enslaved to the elemental spirits of the universe (v. 3) while Gentiles ("you") were enslaved to beings that by nature are not gods (v. 8); the latter are apparently identical to the former (cf. v. 9). Presently they are no longer slaves (v. 7), and Paul urges them not to return to slavery (v. 9; cf. 5:1). For the Gentile Galatians to enter into the Sinai covenant would be to return to slavery. Hagar, a slave whose children are slaves, is the symbol of this covenant (4:21–31). In line with this, Paul can speak of being a slave to the law of sin (Rom 7:25) and being set free from it (8:2).

Because sin is enslavement leading ultimately to death, Paul often personifies sin and death, seeing them as superhuman powers that dominate humans. Thus Paul says in Rom 5:21 that "sin exercised dominion in death." He also speaks of sin exercising dominion in Rom 6:12, and of death doing likewise in Rom 5:14 and 17. Paul refers to being enslaved to sin in Rom 6:6 and elsewhere[18] and of being freed from sin in Rom 6:18 and 22. In Phil 2:7–8 he speaks of Christ's entry into the human situation by saying that Christ took the form of a slave and became obedient unto death.

Paul also refers to sin as enslavement by describing human beings as enslaved to their own impulses. In Rom 16:18 he speaks of being enslaved to one's belly (cf. Titus 2:3; 3:3). In Rom 6:19 he refers to being slaves of impurity.

3. Sin Is Transgression of Law

The idea that sin is transgression of divine law is probably the understanding of sin that comes first to our mind when we hear the word "sin." Paul also understands sin in this way, but for him, this understanding is secondary to understanding sin as idolatry and slavery.[19] It is because one has submitted to something other than God and is now dominated by this false god that one cannot keep the law. For Paul, transgression of the law is the result of sin, not sin in its most basic form.

In some sense one can speak of idolatry as the violation of an implicit law, that one should recognize God as God. In Genesis 3 the refusal to submit to God takes the form of disobeying God's command not to eat the fruit of the tree of knowledge of good and evil. Because of this, Paul refers to Adam's sin as transgression in Rom 5:14 and elsewhere.[20] For Paul, however, "law" specifically means the biblical law, the law God gave the people of Israel through Moses and that is written in the Torah. This is the law

---

18. In Rom 6:16, 17, and 20 Paul speaks of being slaves of sin. In Rom 7:14 he speaks of being sold into slavery under sin.

19. On sin as transgression of law, see Bultmann, *Theology of the New Testament*, 1:246, 249–50, 262–63; Ridderbos, *Paul*, 106–7.

20. In Rom 5:14 Paul uses the word παράβασις; cf. 1 Tim 2:14. In Rom 5:15, 17, and 18 he uses the synonym παράπτωμα.

whose transgression is sin, transgression that cannot be avoided by a human race that has accepted false gods and is enslaved to them.

Paul refers to transgression of the law fairly often. In Rom 5:16 and 20 he refers to the transgressions that followed upon the sin of Adam; in the latter verse, they are specifically transgressions of the law. This is also explicit in Rom 2:23 and elsewhere.[21] In Gal 6:1 Paul speaks of the possibility of transgression among Christians. In Rom 11:11–12 Paul speaks of Israel's unbelief as a transgression. In a number of passages, Paul refers to transgression as that from which the human race needed salvation.[22] For example, in Rom 4:25 Paul says that Jesus

> was handed over to death for our trespasses and raised for our justification.

This is yet another point at which we will misunderstand Paul if we are not careful to avoid presuming that his words mean what we spontaneously understand them to mean. Because we tend to see sin as transgression of divine law, sin is mainly a matter of things we have done wrong. We react with guilt and shame. Paul's extensive discussion of sin can seem to be an oppressive belaboring of our wrongdoing.

However, when Paul speaks of sin, he is mainly thinking about our idolatry and consequent enslavement to sin. Sin is primarily a name for the bad situation in which we find ourselves. We react by longing for freedom.

The Origin of Sin

Paul discusses the origin of sin in Rom 5:12–14.[23] In this passage he says that "sin came into the world through one man, and

---

21. In Rom 2:23 Paul uses the word παράβασις; see also Rom 4:15; Gal 3:19. Paul also speaks of transgressing the law in Rom 2:25, 27; Gal 2:18, using the term παραβάτης.

22. Rom 4:25; 2 Cor 5:19; Eph 1:7; 2:1, 5; Col 2:13. In all of these passages (and in Gal 6:1 and Rom 11:11, 12), Paul uses the word παράπτωμα.

23. On this passage, see Bultmann, *Theology of the New Testament*, 1:250–53; Bornkamm, *Paul*, 123–25; Ridderbos, *Paul*, 95–99.

death came through sin" (v. 12). Paul also speaks about the origin of death in 1 Cor 15:21–22:

> For since death came through a human being, the resurrection of the dead has also come through a human being; for as all die in Adam, so all will be made alive in Christ.

Paul is obviously thinking about Genesis 3 and its depiction of the sin of the first human beings. In these passages he speaks only about the sin of Adam because in both Paul presents Adam as parallel to Christ.

The idea that death, now a universal experience, is the result of Adam's sin implies that it has affected the whole human race. However, Paul states this explicitly in the second half of Rom 5:12, "so death spread to all because all have sinned." This seems to indicate that death—and the sin through which it came—derives both from Adam's sin and from the sin of the human beings who came after him. Paul does not explain how this could be.

The classical explanation is that Adam's sin was transmitted to all other human beings by propagation. This is in line with Paul's emphasis on the importance of Adam's sin but reduces the sin of others simply to their inheritance of Adam's sin. This is not incompatible with what Paul says, but his thought may have lain on other lines. For example, Paul may have thought that all human beings after Adam chose, as Adam had, not to obey God because Adam and Eve provided the only pattern of human life available to them.

In 5:13–14 Paul relates the sin of Adam to the law. In verse 13 he says that sin was in the world before the law, that is, the law of Moses, even though sin is not reckoned as sin when there is no law. But even though sin was not reckoned before the law was given, death reigned from Adam to Moses even over those whose sins were not like the transgression of Adam (v. 14). While Adam transgressed an explicit commandment of God, those who lived between his time and that of Moses did not. Nevertheless, death ruled over them because they also submitted to something other than God and were enslaved by this false god.

Paul here implies that the purpose of the law was not to save Israel from sin.[24] Giving a law to those enslaved to sin would give them no power to keep it. Rather the law would cause sin to be recognized. This would happen not only because it would now be possible to see how far one was aligned with the will of God but also because the explicit statement of God's will provided additional opportunities for sin to cause one to deviate from it. In Rom 5:20 Paul says, "law came in, with the result that the trespass multiplied." He explains how this occurred in Romans 7.

Romans 1:18—3:20

In this passage Paul makes an extensive argument that "all have sinned and fall short of the glory of God" (Rom 3:23). He makes this argument in order to show that both Jew and Gentile need salvation from sin (3:9) and both receive it through faith in Christ; thus there is no reason for Gentiles to become Jews. But this argument entails a demonstration of the universality of sin.

Paul addresses the sinfulness of Gentiles (mainly) in 1:18–32, and that of Jews in 2:17–29. He probably speaks of the sinfulness of both in 2:1–16, though some interpret this passage as having to do only with Jews. In 3:1–8 Paul asks and briefly answers a number of questions raised by the argument he has made in 1:18—2:29; he takes these questions up again in greater detail later in the letter. Finally, in 3:9–20 Paul sums up his argument for the universality of sin.

In addressing the sinfulness of Gentiles, Paul presumes the Jewish perspective that Gentiles are sinners; they are obviously sinners because they do not even know the law of God, much less observe it. But Paul wants to show that Gentiles are culpable sinners; even though God did not give them the law, there was a real possibility that they could have avoided sin.

---

24 On Paul's view of the law, see Bultmann, *Theology of the New Testament*, 1:263–69; H. J. Schoeps, *Paul*, 168–218; Ridderbos, *Paul*, 130–58; Conzelmann, *Outline*, 220–35; Beker, *Paul the Apostle*, 235-54; Fitzymer, "Pauline Teaching," 131–35.

18 For the wrath of God is revealed from heaven against all ungodliness and wickedness of those who by their wickedness suppress the truth. 19 For what can be known about God is plain to them, because God has shown it to them. 20 Ever since the creation of the world his eternal power and divine nature, invisible though they are, have been understood and seen through the things he has made. So they are without excuse; 21 for though they knew God, they did not honor him as God or give thanks to him, but they became futile in their thinking, and their senseless minds were darkened. 22 Claiming to be wise, they became fools; 23 and they exchanged the glory of the immortal God for images resembling a mortal human being or birds or four-footed animals or reptiles.

This argument makes it particularly clear that, for Paul, sin is fundamentally idolatry. Paul says that God revealed to the Gentiles what can be known about God; God's eternal power and divine nature have been understood and seen through the things God made (1:19–20). In other words, God revealed himself to all through his creation. This means that Gentiles have no excuse for not honoring God and giving thanks to God (v. 21) but instead exchanging the glory of the immortal God for images resembling a mortal human being or birds or four-footed animals or reptiles (v. 23). The Gentiles' fundamental mistake was to worship idols.

Even though Paul mainly has Gentiles in mind here, he seems to think that this also applies to Jews. When Paul says in verse 23, "they exchanged the glory of the immortal God for images," he alludes to Ps 106:20, which describes the Israelites' idolatry of the golden calf by saying, "They exchanged the glory of God for the image of an ox that eats grass." In this way Paul hints that Jews are also idolaters, though he does not develop this idea explicitly.

24 Therefore God gave them up in the lusts of their hearts to impurity, to the degrading of their bodies among themselves, 25 because they exchanged the truth about God for a lie and worshiped and served the creature rather than the Creator, who is blessed forever! Amen. 26 For this reason God gave them up to degrading passions. Their women exchanged nat-

56

ural intercourse for unnatural, 27 and in the same way also the men, giving up natural intercourse with women, were consumed with passion for one another. Men committed shameless acts with men and received in their own persons the due penalty for their error. 28 And since they did not see fit to acknowledge God, God gave them up to a debased mind and to things that should not be done. 29 They were filled with every kind of wickedness, evil, covetousness, malice. Full of envy, murder, strife, deceit, craftiness, they are gossips, 30 slanderers, God-haters, insolent, haughty, boastful, inventors of evil, rebellious toward parents, 31 foolish, faithless, heartless, ruthless. 32 They know God's decree, that those who practice such things deserve to die—yet they not only do them but even applaud others who practice them.

The consequence of idolatry, of exchanging the truth about God for a lie and worshiping and serving the creature rather than the Creator (v. 25), of not acknowledging God (v. 28), is that God gave the idolaters up to impurity, to degrading passions, to a debased mind (vv. 24, 26, 28). In other words, idolatry leads to slavery. The idolaters are not enslaved simply to the gods they worship but even more to their own impulses that led them to worship idols rather than God.

God does not deliver idolaters to slavery as a punishment; rather, he permits their free choice to serve idols instead of himself to stand. They make creatures their gods and are enslaved to them. This enslavement manifests itself in homosexual behavior (vv. 26–27) and a long list of vices (vv. 29–31). Paul singles out homosexuality because it shows that enslavement to sin causes people to act in a manner contrary to nature. The exchange of the truth about God for a lie leads to the exchange of natural behavior for unnatural. What is natural is for human beings to worship God. When they depart from nature in this way, other deviations from nature follow.

Paul ends this section with a hint that sin is also transgression of divine law. In 1:32 Paul says the Gentiles do all of these things although they know God's requirement that those who do them deserve to die. While this suggests that sin is a transgression whose punishment is prescribed, Paul does not make it clear how the Gentiles know this requirement of God.

In the following passages, which speak of Jews and Gentiles (2:1–16) and then Jews alone (2:17–29), Paul focuses on sin as transgression of the law. In both passages Paul's basic point is that mere knowledge of right behavior, such as the law provides, does no good unless one behaves properly; and Paul asserts that the people he addresses do not behave properly. Paul seems to presuppose that they cannot behave properly because they have worshiped false gods and so are enslaved to sin, but he does not make this completely explicit.

In 2:1–11 Paul says that all, Jew or Gentile, who judge others condemn themselves because they do the same things they condemn in others.

> 1 Therefore you have no excuse, whoever you are, when you judge others; for in passing judgment on another you condemn yourself, because you, the judge, are doing the very same things. 2 You say, "We know that God's judgment on those who do such things is in accordance with truth." 3 Do you imagine, whoever you are, that when you judge those who do such things and yet do them yourself, you will escape the judgment of God?

Paul does not explain how those who judge others do the same things they condemn in others. Perhaps he means exactly what he says, that is, that anyone who condemns the behavior of another engages in the same behavior. The problem with this explanation is that in fact everyone does not seem to engage in the same bad behavior. Instead Paul might be thinking that the very act of judging another is usurping the place of God and so a form of idolatry. Or Paul might be thinking more generally that even if those who judge others do not sin in the same ways others do, they still fail to do what their superior moral understanding tells them they should.

In 2:12–16 Paul argues that doing, not hearing, the law is crucial.

> 12 All who have sinned apart from the law will also perish apart from the law, and all who have sinned under the law will be judged by the law. 13 For it is not the hearers of the law who are righteous in God's sight, but the doers of the law who will be justified. 14 When Gentiles, who do not possess the law, do instinctively what the law requires, these, though not having

the law, are a law to themselves. 15 They show that what the
law requires is written on their hearts, to which their own conscience also bears witness; and their conflicting thoughts will
accuse or perhaps excuse them 16 on the day when, according
to my gospel, God, through Jesus Christ, will judge the secret
thoughts of all.

Paul makes this point by saying that a Gentile who kept the
law without knowing it would be found righteous on the day of
judgment (vv. 14–16). It seems clear from Paul's overall argument
that he considers this an unrealized possibility; he is arguing for the
universality of sin. But the existence of the possibility shows that
keeping the law is essential. In the following section (2:17–29), Paul
makes this point explicitly concerning Jews.

17 But if you call yourself a Jew and rely on the law and boast
of your relation to God 18 and know his will and determine
what is best because you are instructed in the law, 19 and if you
are sure that you are a guide to the blind, a light to those who
are in darkness, 20 a corrector of the foolish, a teacher of children, having in the law the embodiment of knowledge and
truth, 21 you, then, that teach others, will you not teach yourself? While you preach against stealing, do you steal? 22 You
that forbid adultery, do you commit adultery? You that abhor
idols, do you rob temples? 23 You that boast in the law, do you
dishonor God by breaking the law? 24 For, as it is written,
"The name of God is blasphemed among the Gentiles because
of you."

In verses 21–22 Paul accuses Jews of breaking the law by asking, "While you preach against stealing, do you steal? You that forbid adultery, do you commit adultery? You that abhor idols, do you
rob temples?" Paul obviously thinks the answer to these questions
is "Yes," because he summarizes them by saying in verse 23 that
Jews "dishonor God by breaking the law."

Paul's third question concerns the sin of idolatry. But instead
of simply saying, as he does in the other questions, that Jews do
what they condemn in others, in this case he says that they rob temples even though they abhor idolatry. The logic of Paul's argument
requires that robbing temples be equivalent to idolatry. Paul may

mention the idolatry of Israel in this indirect way because of his concern in Romans to safeguard the prerogatives of Israel. Robbing temples might mean taking things from the temples of idols, which would be seen as participation in the worship of such idols. Or it might mean profanation of the Jerusalem temple, which would be seen as idolatry.

In 2:25–29 Paul again makes the point that acting in accordance with the law, not simply having the law, is what is important. He refers again to the possibility that a Gentile keep the precepts of the law. Once again it seems clear from Paul's overall argument that he considers this an unrealized possibility.

After touching briefly on a series of matters arising from the argument he has just made (3:1–8), Paul sums up the argument in 3:9–20. He makes use of a catena of ten quotations from Scripture to show the utter sinfulness of all human beings (vv. 10–18). Paul ends by referring again to the relationship between law and sin. Through the law comes knowledge of sin (v. 20).

III.
SALVATION

We have explored Paul's conception of God and seen that Paul understands human beings as needing salvation because they have not recognized God as God but instead have given the honor and glory due God to something other than God. This idolatry has enslaved them to the false gods they worshiped, and made them transgressors of God's law. We now begin to consider the way God has saved human beings from this situation according to Paul.

A. SALVATION AS A FREE GIFT

When Paul begins to reflect on God's salvation of the human race in his Letter to the Romans, the first major point he makes is that this salvation is a free gift, issuing from God's love of the human race. We will discuss this section of Romans below. Paul's view that salvation is a free gift, not based on anything humans do to earn it, is summed up succinctly in Eph 2:5:

By grace you have been saved.[1]

The gratuity of salvation is implied by Paul's understanding of the human situation. If the human predicament is one of enslavement to sin, then human beings cannot do anything other than serve sin as their master. Since human beings can do nothing to attain salvation, salvation must be provided freely if it is to happen at all.[2]

---

1. On "grace," see Bultmann, *Theology of the New Testament*, 1:288–92; Bornkamm, *Paul*, 139–41; Conzelmann, *Outline*, 213–14; Beker, *Paul the Apostle*, 264–67; Dunn, *Theology of Paul*, 319–23.

2. A similar idea is presented by the parable of Jesus found in Matt 18:23–35. In this parable the relationship of human beings to God is compared to that of a slave to his master. The slave owed his master an enormous debt that he could not repay, and his debt was forgiven by the master.

The gratuity of salvation is also implied by Paul's view that salvation does not come from keeping the law. If it were possible for someone to achieve salvation, surely this would occur as a result of keeping God's law. But if salvation does not come from keeping God's law, there can be no other kind of activity that would lead to salvation.

We speak about the gratuity of salvation when we consider salvation as God's action. Considering salvation from the perspective of human action leads us to speak of faith. Faith is the human acceptance of the gratuitous offer of salvation.[3]

Experientially, faith is acceptance of the message about Christ.

> So faith comes from what is heard, and what is heard comes through the word of Christ. (Rom 10:17)

But this is much more than an intellectual acknowledgment of its truth, which is the understanding of faith that might come first to our minds. It is assent to its truth and to the consequences of its being true. Seen more deeply, faith is a union with Christ that sets the human race free from sin. It is simultaneously release from slavery to sin and acknowledgment of God as God. Thus faith can be described as obedience (Rom 1:5; 2 Cor 9:13), obedience that is the opposite of the disobedience involved in sin. Immediately before the passage quoted above, Paul says,

> not all have obeyed the good news. (Rom 10:16)

Faith is not only an act of the intellect; it is also an act of the will.

In Rom 3:22 and other places,[4] Paul uses a phrase that is usually translated "faith *in* Jesus Christ" but literally reads, "faith *of* Jesus Christ." In recent years a number of scholars have argued that the literal rendering gives the correct meaning of the phrase.[5] If this is

---

3. On faith, see Bultmann, *Theology of the New Testament*, 1:314–24; Bornkamm, *Paul*, 141–46; Ridderbos, *Paul*, 231–52; Conzelmann, *Outline*, 171–73; Beker, *Paul the Apostle*, 267–69; Fitzmyer, "Pauline Teaching," 137–38; Dunn, *Theology of Paul*, 371–85.

4. See Gal 2:16; 3:22. Rom 3:26 has "faith of Jesus"; Gal 2:20, "faith of the son of God"; Eph 3:12, "his faith"; and Phil 3:9, "faith of Christ."

5. E.g., S. K. Williams, "Again *Pistis Christou*"; R. B. Hays, *The Faith of Jesus Christ*.

right, at least when he uses this phrase, Paul is emphasizing the saving significance of Jesus' own faith rather than that of those who follow him. The faith of his followers resembles that of Jesus himself. But more than that, by dying and rising with Christ, the followers of Jesus participate in his faith; his faith becomes theirs to some degree.

Paul's view that salvation is a free gift that human beings freely accept becomes more complicated when Paul considers the rejection of salvation by some Jews. Because this seems to suggest that human beings can prevent God from keeping the promise to save Israel (see Rom 9:6), Paul argues that God is the cause of unbelief even though it remains a human responsibility (Rom 9:6–24). Paul offers no explicit explanation of this. What he may be thinking is that unbelief is a continuation of human sinfulness that derives from the free choice of humans. Thus, if God does not rescue some human beings from sin, their plight is their own responsibility. Paul argues, however, that it is only for the sake of some greater good that God does not offer salvation to someone. We will consider Paul's understanding of God's mysterious plan for Israel when we discuss the future aspect of "Salvation as New Life with Christ."

Three hundred years after the time of Paul, the Pelagian controversy provided an occasion for Augustine (354–430) to think more deeply about the relationship between grace and free will.[6] Following Paul closely but developing Paul's thought, Augustine argued that grace and free will are simultaneously operative both in belief (§§ 28–37) and unbelief (§§ 41–45). In the former case, Augustine says, grace helps human beings to will and then helps them when they will. In the latter, God either turns the wills of human beings toward evil in line with their previous inclination toward it or simply does not turn them to good.

Augustine develops these ideas in order to reject the Pelagian position that the law is the free gift of God that humans obey by means of free will (§§ 22–24) or even that human nature is the free gift of God by which human beings are able to live well (§ 25). Augustine acknowledges that some parts of Scripture say that eternal life is the reward of good works (e.g., Matt 16:27), whereas the

---

6. See Augustine, "On Grace and Free Will," in Meeks, *The Writings of St. Paul*, 220–36.

letters of Paul say that it is the free gift of God. But Augustine rejects the Pelagian reconciliation of these two. Instead Augustine argues that grace and free will are simultaneously operative in good works (§§ 19–23). In this he goes beyond anything explicit in Paul but in a direction congenial to Paul's thought.

Plan of Salvation

In discussing Paul's understanding of God, we have noted that Paul sees God as having a plan.[7] Here we observe that God's plan was salvation of the human race as a free gift and reflect on the plan in more detail.

Paul refers in very general terms to God's plan to save the human race from sin—when, for example, he speaks of God's "plan" (πρόθεσις),[8] or God's "predestination" (προορίζω) of the salvation of Christians,[9] or the fullness of time (Gal 4:4) in which salvation came. In 1 Cor 2:7 Paul says that God predestined a wisdom hidden in a mystery for our glory.

> But we speak God's wisdom, secret and hidden, which God decreed before the ages for our glory.

This mystery is salvation through the death of Christ (1 Cor 2:1–2).[10] It had been kept secret for long ages but has now been revealed (Rom 16:25).[11] Such ideas reflect the influence of the apocalyptic emphasis on God's sovereign control of history. Paul stresses that God's plan was a mystery partly because it was so unexpected by him and others that someone like Jesus be the Christ and that the plight of the human race be what Jesus' messiahship revealed it to be.

---

7. On this topic, see Schoeps, *Paul*, 229–58; Fitzmyer, *Paul and His Theology*, 44–48.

8. See Rom 8:28; 9:11; Eph 1:11; 3:11; cf. 2 Tim 1:9. See also the discussion of God as sovereign, above.

9. See Rom 8:29, 30; 1 Cor 2:7; Eph 1:5, 11.

10. Cf. also Eph 1:9; 1 Tim 3:16.

11. See also Eph 3:9; Col 1:26. See N. A. Dahl, "Form-Critical Observations on Early Christian Preaching."

Two related things cause Paul to reflect somewhat more specifically on God's plan of salvation as it has unfolded through history up to the time of Jesus: first, his thoughts about the origin of sin, and second, the need to arrive at a new understanding of the purpose of the law. The two are combined in Rom 5:13–14.

> 13 sin was indeed in the world before the law, but sin is not reckoned when there is no law. 14 Yet death exercised dominion from Adam to Moses, even over those whose sins were not like the transgression of Adam, who is a type of the one who was to come.

Here Paul speaks about a period of human history between Adam and Moses in which sin dominated the human race through death even though the law had not been given. This suggests two further periods, though Paul does not name them explicitly: a period from Moses to Christ, and the period of Christ.[12]

Paul speaks most directly of God's plan of salvation in Gal 3:6–4:11. In this passage Paul's point is that Gentile Christians should not keep the Jewish law. But he makes this point by offering an interpretation of God's dealing with the people of Israel, which is the vehicle by which God saved the human race.

This passage suggests that God's first step in saving the human race from sin was to call Abraham. Abraham's response to God's call was that he

> believed God, and it was reckoned to him as righteousness.
> (Gal 3:6, quoting Gen 15:6)

In the same way, everyone else, both Jew and Gentile, would become righteous, that is, free from sin, by believing. These are the children of Abraham (Gal 3:7). Abraham is the model for everyone else who would be saved. Paul explains the exemplary character of Abraham more fully in Romans 4, as we will see.

Paul, however, not only thinks that Abraham is the model of the person who is saved from sin; he also thinks that God promised Abraham to save all nations from sin through his offspring. This

---

12. Fitzmyer, *Paul and His Theology*, 45.

promise, which can also be called a covenant (Gal 3:15–17), was stated in different ways in the Bible; Paul may have in mind, most of all, God's saying to Abraham in Gen 22:18 that

> by your offspring shall all the nations of the earth gain blessing for themselves.

This promise to Abraham was fulfilled by the coming of Christ, who is the promised offspring of Abraham (Gal 3:16, 19). The law, given 430 years after this promise, does not add to it or annul it (Gal 3:15, 17). Thus the law—and the Sinai covenant of which it is a part—is not an element of God's plan of salvation that is comparable to the covenant with Abraham. It is part of the plan but does not change the plan contained in God's covenant with Abraham.

What, then, was the purpose of the law? Paul explains that it was temporary, intended to last only until the promised offspring of Abraham arrived, that is, Christ.

> Why then the law? It was added because of transgressions, until the offspring would come to whom the promise had been made. (Gal 3:19)

The purpose of the law was to imprison all things under the power of sin (Gal 3:22–23). What this means, as we have seen, is that the law increased the already existing slavery of the human race to sin and death, in order to prepare for the coming of salvation.

In addition to reflecting on the operation of the plan of God in past and present, Paul also reflects on its future unfolding. We will discuss this in "Salvation as New Life with Christ."

Romans 3:21—4:25

In Rom 1:18—3:20 Paul established the universal need for salvation, that is, the universality of sin. In 3:21—4:25 he begins to present the good news that God offers freedom from sin to all through Jesus Christ, a presentation that will occupy the remainder of the body of Romans. The point Paul is making to the Romans is that freedom from sin does not come from the law. In making this argument, however, Paul also shows that he understands salvation as a free gift.

In 3:21–22 and 25–26 Paul speaks of God's salvation of the human race from sin as a revelation of God's righteousness.

> 21 But now, apart from law, the righteousness of God has been disclosed, and is attested by the law and the prophets, 22 the righteousness of God through faith in Jesus Christ for all who believe. For there is no distinction, 23 since all have sinned and fall short of the glory of God; 24 they are now justified by his grace as a gift, through the redemption that is in Christ Jesus, 25 whom God put forward as a sacrifice of atonement by his blood, effective through faith. He did this to show his righteousness, because in his divine forbearance he had passed over the sins previously committed; 26 it was to prove at the present time that he himself is righteous and that he justifies the one who has faith in Jesus.

Salvation reveals God's righteousness because through it God both keeps the promises of salvation found in the law and the prophets (v. 21) and sets right the alienation of the human race from God through sin (vv. 25–26). As a result, human beings are made righteous, or justified (v. 24). This is an image of salvation that we will discuss below in considering the way dying and rising with Christ set Christians free from sin.

In 3:22 and 26 Paul says that this salvation is given to all those who believe in Jesus Christ or, according to some scholars, who have the faith of Jesus Christ. In either interpretation of Paul's statements, but especially the latter, this faith is not primarily a matter of adherence to a system of beliefs, or an emotion, or faithfulness to an organization. Rather faith is a matter of seeing what God has done for Christians through Jesus and willingly associating oneself with it. It is the acceptance of what God has done through Jesus to right what is wrong. It is the opposite of sin.

In 3:24 Paul says that being made righteous through the redemption that is in Christ Jesus is a free gift. Paul develops this point in 3:27–31 by arguing that boasting is excluded.

If salvation came through Christians' own efforts, particularly their efforts to keep the law of God, they could boast of their achievement. But since their salvation is a free gift, accepted by faith, they have nothing they can boast about. Paul concludes by saying that this perspective is not incompatible with the law but rather upholds the law (v. 31). Paul supports this assertion in Romans 4 by arguing at length that the law itself, in its portrayal of Abraham, teaches that salvation is a free gift, accepted by faith.

> 1 What then are we to say was gained by Abraham, our ancestor according to the flesh? 2 For if Abraham was justified by works, he has something to boast about, but not before God. 3 For what does the scripture say? "Abraham believed God, and it was reckoned to him as righteousness." 4 Now to one who works, wages are not reckoned as a gift but as something due. 5 But to one who without works trusts him who justifies the ungodly, such faith is reckoned as righteousness. 6 So also David speaks of the blessedness of those to whom God reckons righteousness apart from works: 7 "Blessed are those whose iniquities are forgiven, and whose sins are covered; 8 blessed is the one against whom the Lord will not reckon sin."

Paul bases this argument on Gen 15:6, "Abraham believed in God and it was reckoned to him as righteousness"—the same text he uses in Galatians 3. In Rom 4:3–8 he argues that the word "reckoned" means that righteousness was given to Abraham as a free gift of God, not as something he had earned. Paul supports this by quoting Ps 32:1–2, in which the word "reckon" is used as synonymous with forgiveness of sins. This is the negative counterpart of reckoning someone righteous.

In Rom 4:9–12 Paul goes on to point out that Abraham believed and was reckoned righteous before he was circumcised.

> 9 Is this blessedness, then, pronounced only on the circumcised, or also on the uncircumcised? We say, "Faith was reckoned to Abraham as righteousness." 10 How then was it reckoned to him? Was it before or after he had been circumcised? It was not after, but before he was circumcised. 11 He received the sign of circumcision as a seal of the righteousness that he had by faith while he was still uncircumcised. The purpose was to make him the ancestor of all who believe without being circumcised and who thus have righteousness reckoned

to them, 12 and likewise the ancestor of the circumcised who
are not only circumcised but who also follow the example of
the faith that our ancestor Abraham had before he was circumcised.

Abraham's believing and being reckoned righteous is narrated
in Genesis 15; his circumcision is narrated in Genesis 17. Since
Abraham had already been reckoned righteous before being circumcised, his circumcision was a seal of that righteousness (v. 11).
Because of this, Abraham is father of all the uncircumcised who
believe and arc reckoned righteous and of the circumcised who
believe as Abraham did while still uncircumcised (vv. 11–12). All
believers, both Jew and Gentile, have righteousness reckoned to
them as a free gift following the example of Abraham.

In 4:13–17, by arguing that righteousness comes from faith,
not the law, Paul supports the argument that righteousness does
not come to Abraham or his descendants through circumcision.

13 For the promise that he would inherit the world did not
come to Abraham or to his descendants through the law but
through the righteousness of faith. 14 If it is the adherents of
the law who are to be the heirs, faith is null and the promise is
void. 15 For the law brings wrath; but where there is no law,
neither is there violation. 16 For this reason it depends on
faith, in order that the promise may rest on grace and be guar-
anteed to all his descendants, not only to the adherents of the
law but also to those who share the faith of Abraham (for he is
the father of all of us, 17 as it is written, "I have made you the
father of many nations")—in the presence of the God in whom
he believed, who gives life to the dead and calls into existence
the things that do not exist.

If righteousness came from keeping the law, it would not
come through faith, and the promise made to Abraham would be
nullified (v. 14). Righteousness comes through faith in order to
keep the promise of salvation as a free gift, intended for both Jew
and Gentile (v. 16). The latter fulfills Gen 17:5, in which God
said to Abraham, "I have made you the father of many nations"
(Rom 4:17).

In 4:18–22 Paul describes the faith of Abraham in more detail.

18 Hoping against hope, he believed that he would become "the father of many nations," according to what was said, "So numerous shall your descendants be." 19 He did not weaken in faith when he considered his own body, which was already as good as dead (for he was about a hundred years old), or when he considered the barrenness of Sarah's womb. 20 No distrust made him waver concerning the promise of God, but he grew strong in his faith as he gave glory to God, 21 being fully convinced that God was able to do what he had promised. 22 Therefore his faith "was reckoned to him as righteousness."

In 4:17 Paul describes God as one "who gives life to the dead and calls into existence the things that do not exist." Abraham believed God's promise to make him the father of many nations even though he had no children and was himself as good as dead and his wife was barren (vv. 18–19). Despite the lack of obvious means to do so, Abraham believed that God would do what he promised, and this faith was reckoned to him as righteousness (vv. 20–22).

Finally, Paul says that Abraham's faith is a model for that of Christians (4:23–25). Like Abraham Christians believe in God, who gives life to the dead and calls into existence the things that do not exist. They believe that God raised Jesus from the dead. Jesus died for their trespasses and was raised to make them righteous, bringing into existence a righteousness that had not previously existed.

B. THE PERSON OF CHRIST (CHRISTOLOGY)

God offers the free gift of salvation to the human race through Christ. At no point in his letters does Paul discuss the person of Christ at any length as a topic of its own. Of course, Paul constantly refers to Christ, and his understanding of the person of Christ is implied everywhere. It is implied by various titles Paul uses for Christ, particularly the titles "Christ," "Son of God," and "Lord."[1] It is also implied by the parallels Paul establishes between Christ and God.

Christ

In line with Paul's own usage, we have been using "Christ" as simply a name for Jesus.[2] However, it is actually a title. It is the Greek translation of the Hebrew title "Messiah," which means "anointed." Thus Jesus Christ means Jesus the Messiah, or Jesus the Anointed One.

Paul himself surely understands this. One indication is that Paul alternates between speaking of Jesus Christ and Christ Jesus. We find the former eighty times in the Pauline Letters, including Rom 1:4, where Paul refers to

Jesus Christ our Lord.

We find the latter eighty-nine times, including Rom 1:1, where Paul refers to himself as

Paul, a servant of Christ Jesus.

---

1. On the Christology of Paul and other early Christians, see Callan, *The Origins of Christian Faith*.

2. On this title, see Dahl, "The Messiahship of Jesus in Paul" in *Jesus the Christ*, 15-25; Dunn, *Theology of Paul*, 197–99.

This seems to show that Paul knows "Christ" is a title attached to the name Jesus, not simply a part of the name. Similarly, Paul applies other titles to the name Jesus, not to Christ. Thus in Rom 10:9 Paul says that one confesses that Jesus is Lord, not that Christ is Lord.

> If you confess with your lips that Jesus is Lord and believe in your heart that God raised him from the dead, you will be saved.

And finally, in Rom 9:5 Paul says that the Christ derives from the people of Israel according to the flesh.

> to them belong the patriarchs, and from them, according to the flesh, comes the Christ, who is over all, God blessed forever. Amen.

Since this is the last in a series of blessings given by God to the people of Israel, this seems to show that Paul here sees "Christ" as meaning the Messiah, the Savior promised by God.

Even though Paul understands what is meant by "Christ," he does not seem to expect his addressees to understand what it means. It is possible to understand everything Paul says about "Christ" without knowing the meaning of the term. In his letters Paul simply uses "Christ" as a name for Jesus, much as we do today.

Paul's very frequent use of "Christ" without relying on it to communicate anything about Jesus probably means that at a very early point in Christian history, the title "Christ" was so important to faith in Jesus and so closely associated with him that it became virtually part of his name. Among Jewish followers of Jesus, it was very meaningful; among Gentiles, it was not. The term "Christ" could only become meaningful to Gentiles when accompanied by education about Israel's hopes and the language used to express them. Since there were other titles that communicated more directly to Gentiles, for example, "Son of God" and "Lord," these were used to impart the significance of Jesus to them. "Christ" continued to be used, however, even when it no longer served to convey who Jesus was, because of its fundamental historical importance.

Among Jesus' earliest Jewish followers, saying that Jesus was the Christ/Messiah meant that he was the eschatological bringer of salvation promised by God to Israel. He was the fulfillment of a hope developed in the context of apocalyptic thought. The coming of Jesus as the Christ/Messiah meant that the end times had begun, the time at which God would keep the promise to save Israel and the rest of the world from all evil. Even though Paul does not use the title "Christ" to convey this about Jesus, it is how he understands Jesus. This will become clear in the discussion of "The Action of Christ."

Their belief that Jesus was the Christ confronted the earliest followers of Jesus with the problem that Jesus had not obviously accomplished salvation. He had not completely eradicated evil from the world and established justice and peace under the sovereignty of God. Their solution to this was the expectation that Jesus would come a second time to complete the accomplishment of salvation. With the first coming of Jesus, the end times had already begun; the end times, however, would not be complete until Jesus comes a second time. Paul shares the expectation of a second coming of Jesus at which Jesus will do all that the Christ was expected to do.

Son of God and Lord

1. Pre-Pauline Use

The pre-Pauline church employed the titles "Son of God" and "Lord" both because of their use during Jesus' lifetime and because they were implied by recognition of Jesus as Christ after his death and resurrection.

In the gospels Jesus is called Lord by those asking for his help and by his disciples (two groups that are not entirely separate). We find the former in Mark 7:28/Matt 15:27 and elsewhere,[3] and the latter in Mark 11:3/Matt 21:3/Luke 19:31 and elsewhere.[4] In Mark 7:28 the Syrophoenician woman asks Jesus to cure her daughter:

---

3. See Matt 8:2/Luke 5:12; Matt 8:6, 8/Luke 7:6; Matt 9:28; 15:22, 25; 17:15; 20:30, 31, 33/Luke 18:41; John 4:49; 5:7.

4. See Matt 7:21–22/Luke 6:46; Matt 8:21/Luke 9:59; Matt 8:25; 14:28, 30; 16:22; 17:4; 18:21; 26:22; Luke 5:8; 9:54, 61; 10:17, 40; 11:1; 12:41; 13:23; 17:37;

Lord, even the dogs under the table eat the children's crumbs.

In Mark 11:3 Jesus tells his disciples to explain why they are taking a colt by saying,

The Lord needs it and will send it back here immediately.

Likewise, in the gospels Jesus calls God his Father and less often speaks about himself as Son or Son of God. We find the former in Mark 13:32/Matt 24:36 and elsewhere,[5] and both in Matt 11:25–27/Luke 10:21–22.

> 25 At that time Jesus said, "I thank you, Father, Lord of heaven and earth, because you have hidden these things from the wise and the intelligent and have revealed them to infants; 26 yes, Father, for such was your gracious will. 27 All things have been handed over to me by my Father; and no one knows the Son except the Father, and no one knows the Father except the Son and anyone to whom the Son chooses to reveal him."
>
> (Matt 11:25–27)

Although the gospel traditions have probably been influenced by the belief of Christians that Jesus is Lord and Son of God, it is completely plausible that these titles were used for Jesus during his life. It would have been natural for those seeking Jesus' help and for his disciples to acknowledge his rightful authority over them by referring to him as Lord. And it would have been very natural for Jesus to refer to God as his Father and himself as Son of God because the people of Israel understood themselves as children of God.

Use of "Lord" and "Son of God" for Jesus during his lifetime made it easy to continue using these titles for Jesus after his death and resurrection. But the belief that Jesus was the Messiah, based on his resurrection, was a more important reason for continued use

---

19:8; 22:33, 38, 49; John 4:11, 15, 19; 6:34, 68; 9:36, 38; 11:3, 12, 21, 27, 32, 34, 39; 13:6, 9, 13, 25, 36, 37; 14:5, 8, 22; 20:18, 25, 28; 21:7, 15–17, 20–21.

5. See Mark 14:36/Matt 26:39/Luke 22:42; Matt 7:21; 10:32–33; 12:50; 15:13; 16:17; 18:10, 14, 19, 35; 20:23; 26:29, 42, 53; Luke 2:49; 22:29; 23:34, 46; 24:49; John 2:16; 3:35; 4:21, 23; and many other passages.

of these titles. The Messiah was the eschatological king, and the king is one of those for whom the title "Lord" is most appropriate. We can see that the king is also lord in Ps 110:1. This psalm originally applied to the king of Israel. The psalmist begins,

> The Lord [i.e., God] says to my lord [i.e., the king]....

When this psalm was understood as a prediction fulfilled by Jesus as Messiah, it also implied that Jesus is Lord. This connection is visible in Mark 12:35–37 and parallels.

> 35 While Jesus was teaching in the temple, he said, "How can the scribes say that the Messiah is the son of David? 36 David himself, by the Holy Spirit, declared, 'The Lord said to my Lord, "Sit at my right hand, until I put your enemies under your feet."' 37 David himself calls him Lord; so how can he be his son?"

Just as the king of Israel was appropriately called "lord," so he was appropriately called son of God. We can see that the king was also son of God in Ps 2:7 and 2 Sam 7:14. The former, originally addressed to the king of Israel, says,

> You are my son, today I have begotten you.

In the latter, the prophet Nathan, speaking for God, promises David concerning his offspring,

> I will be his father, and he shall be my son.

When these passages were understood as predictions fulfilled by Jesus as Messiah, they also implied that Jesus is Son of God. This connection is visible in Heb 1:1–5, where both passages are seen as addressed to Jesus.

Thus in pre-Pauline Christianity "Lord" and "Son of God" were synonymous with "Christ." "Son of God" emphasizes the Christ's relationship with God; "Lord" emphasizes the Christ's relationship with believers. "Lord" is a self-involving designation; the one who uses it declares acceptance of the authority of Jesus.

2. Importance for Paul

Unlike the title "Christ," which was used exclusively by Jews, the titles "lord" and "son of God" were also used by Gentiles. And the meaning of these titles for Gentiles was approximately the same as their basic meaning for Jews. Among Gentiles "lord" expressed the rightful authority of a superior and was used for both human beings and gods. "Son of god" expressed a special relationship to one of the gods and was used for divine and semidivine offspring of the gods, including Roman emperors from Augustus onward.

Use of these titles by Gentiles with approximately the same meaning they had for Jews made these titles very useful for Paul and others who proclaimed Christ to the Gentiles. Paul speaks of Jesus as Lord in about two hundred passages.[6] He speaks of Jesus as Son of God less frequently, though still fairly often. Paul calls Jesus Son of God in several passages,[7] including Rom 1:4, where he also refers to Jesus as Lord. Here Paul says that Jesus

> was declared to be Son of God with power according to the spirit of holiness by resurrection from the dead, Jesus Christ our Lord.

Elsewhere Paul refers to Jesus as "his Son," where "God" is the antecedent of "his,"[8] or simply as "Son" (1 Cor 15:28). Paul also speaks of God as Father of Jesus in Rom 15:6 and elsewhere.[9]

Gentile use of these titles for rulers corresponded closely to Jewish use of them for the Messiah, the eschatological king. Jews also used "Lord" as a title for God, corresponding to Gentile use of it as a title for gods. Gentile use of "son of god" as a title for divinities, however, had no counterpart in Jewish usage. Especially among Gentiles, the use of these titles for Christ tended to make Christ comparable to the divinities of the Hellenistic world. Thus

---

6. This is Dunn's estimate (*Theology of Paul*, 244 n 47).

7. See 2 Cor 1:19; Gal 2:20; Eph 4:13.

8. See Rom 1:3, 9; 5:10; 8:3, 29, 32; 1 Cor 1:9; Gal 1:16; 4:4, 6; 1 Thess 1:10; Col 1:13.

9. See 2 Cor 1:3; 11:31; Eph 1:3; Col 1:3.

Christ was acclaimed "Lord"[10] as gods were acclaimed "Lord" in the Hellenistic world.

This tended to reveal new dimensions of what it meant for Jesus to be the Messiah. Seeing Jesus as Lord and Son of God in Hellenistic terms added to the expectation of Jesus' future second coming a focus on his present enthronement in heaven, reigning over heaven and earth at God's right hand. This was an additional way in which the end times were already present. Not only had the Messiah appeared; he already reigned, though his reign was not yet visible to all. And focus on the present reign of Jesus added to the expectation of his future full establishment of the kingdom of God an emphasis on his present conquest of the spiritual powers of evil (1 Cor 15:24–28; Eph 1:20–23).

> 24 Then comes the end, when he hands over the kingdom to God the Father, after he has destroyed every ruler and every authority and power. 25 For he must reign until he has put all his enemies under his feet. (1 Cor 15:24–25)

Even in view of these new dimensions of Jesus' messiahship, calling Jesus Lord and Son of God did not mean exactly the same thing for Christians that it meant for Gentiles in general. Paul indicates the difference between the two in 1 Cor 8:5–6. Here Paul acknowledges that many gods and many lords are recognized in the Hellenistic world. But

> for us there is one God, the Father…and one Lord, Jesus Christ.

Christ is a lord like the lords recognized by the Gentiles, but Christ is the only Lord recognized by Christians. Others are not their lords.

3. Preexistence

In 1 Cor 8:6 Paul describes the Lord Jesus Christ as the one

through whom are all things and through whom we exist.[11]

---

10. See Rom 10:9; 1 Cor 12:3; Phil 2:11.
11. On preexistence, see Ridderbos, *Paul*, 68–86; Dunn, *Theology of Paul*, 266–93.

In the previous verse Paul described God, the Father, as the one "from whom are all things." Taken together with the latter statement, the statement that Christ is the one "through whom are all things" implies that Christ was the agent through whom God created the universe. And this in turn implies that Christ existed at the beginning of creation, before his birth as a human being. Other passages that express the same view include Phil 2:6–11, 2 Cor 8:9, and Col 1:15–20. The first of these begins by speaking of Jesus as one

> 6 who, though he was in the form of God, did not regard equality with God as something to be exploited, 7 but emptied himself, taking the form of a slave, being born in human likeness. (Phil 2:6–7a)

In part this view probably derives from other implications of the Hellenistic meaning of the titles "lord" and "son of god." Hellenistic use of these titles for gods may have helped suggest that, like them, Jesus was eternally Lord and Son of God.

Although Paul speaks of the preexistence of Jesus, he does not develop this view very fully, and it does not seem to be important for his understanding of Jesus as Messiah. As we will see in "The Action of Christ," Paul sees Jesus as performing the work of the Messiah primarily through his death and resurrection.

The Parallel between Christ and God

An even more exalted view of Jesus is implicit in Paul's frequent statements about Christ that are the same as, or similar to, his statements about God. The basis for these statements may be indicated in Col 1:19; 2:9, where Paul says that the fullness dwelt in Christ.[12]

> For in him the whole fullness of deity dwells bodily. (Col 2:9)

Christ is the one in and through whom God acts, accomplishing the salvation God promised. This has far-reaching implications for Paul's

---

12. See Dunn, *Theology of Paul*, 204–6.

understanding of Christ, but Paul does not develop them explicitly.[13] Like his understanding of the preexistence of Christ, this does not play an important role in Paul's explicit presentation of the significance of Christ. There are parallels between Paul's statements about Christ and Paul's statements about God in himself, about God in relation to others and how human beings should relate to God.

1. Christ and God in Himself

In 1 Cor 8:6 Paul says that there is one God,

> from whom are all things and for whom we exist, and one Lord Jesus Christ, through whom are all things and through whom we exist.

Just as there is one God, so there is one Lord.[14] The relationship between them is not explained. The one God, however, is the Creator of all and the one for whom Christians exist; the one Lord is the one through whom all things, and Christians in particular, came to be. In Rom 11:36 Paul says that God is the one through whom are all things; this is said of Christ in 1 Cor 8:6.

- The spirit of God   is also the spirit of Christ (Rom 8:9; Gal 4:6).
- As God has glory,   so does Christ (2 Cor 4:4).[15]
- As God is loving,   so is Christ (Rom 8:35).[16]

The love of God is in Christ (Rom 8:39). Christ is the power and wisdom of God (1 Cor 1:24). Paul also mentions the power of Christ in 2 Cor 12:9. The salutations of Paul's letters regularly wish that the recipients may have grace and peace from God and Jesus.[17] For example, in Rom 1:7 Paul says,

---

13. Schoeps explicates these implications (*Paul*, 149–60).

14. 1 Tim 2:4 says that just as there is one God, so there is one mediator, Jesus Christ.

15. See also 2 Cor 8:23; 2 Thess 2:14.

16. See also Gal 2:20; Eph 3:19; 5:25; 6:23.

17. Rom 1:7; 1 Cor 1:3; 2 Cor 1:2; Gal 1:3; Eph 1:2; Phil 1:2; 2 Thess 1:2; cf. 1 Tim 1:2; 2 Tim 1:2; Titus 1:4; Phlm 3. The salutations of 1 and 2 Timothy add a

Grace to you and peace from God our Father and the Lord
Jesus Christ.

In Rom 5:1 Paul speaks of having peace with God through Christ.
Paul also regularly ends his letters with a wish that the recipients
may have grace from Christ.[18] For example, Rom 16:20 reads,

The grace of our Lord Jesus Christ be with you.

2. Christ and God in Relation to Others

We noted above that Christ was the agent of God in creation.

- Just as God saved Christians,   so Christ is Savior (Phil 3:20).[19]
- As Christians form the   they form the congregation
  congregation of God,   of Christ (Rom 16:16).
- Through and in Christ   God reconciled people to himself
     (2 Cor 5:18–19; cf. Rom 5:11).
- Through Christ   God destined people for sonship
     (Eph 1:5) and salvation
     (1 Thess 5:19).
- Through Christ   God gives Christians victory
     (1 Cor 15:57) and will raise them
     from the dead (1 Thess 4:14).
- Through Jesus Christ   God will judge (Rom 2:16).
- Just as all will stand before the   so all will stand before the
  judgment seat of God   judgment seat of Christ
  (Rom 14:10),   (2 Cor 5:10; cf. 2 Tim 4:1).

When Christ brings to light the things now hidden in darkness,
each will receive commendation from God (1 Cor 4:5). The king-

---

wish for mercy to the wishes for grace and peace. In Eph 6:23 Paul wishes that the
recipients of the letter may have peace from God and Jesus. Paul also parallels the
grace of God and that of Christ in Rom 5:15 and 2 Thess 1:12.

18. Rom 16:20; 1 Cor 16:23; 2 Cor 13:13; Gal 6:18; Phil 4:23; 1 Thess 5:28; Phlm
25. Paul also refers to the grace of Christ in 2 Cor 8:9 and Gal 1:6.

19. See also Eph 5:23; cf. 2 Tim 1:10; Titus 1:4; 2:13; 3:6. 1 Tim 1:15 says that
Christ came into the world to save sinners.

dom of God is also the kingdom of Christ,[20] which Christ will hand over to God at the end (1 Cor 15:24).

3. Others in Relation to Christ and God

- Just as it is necessary to believe in God,

  it is necessary to believe in Christ (Gal 2:16).[21]

- Just as every tongue confesses God (Rom 14:11),

  so every tongue confesses Jesus (Phil 2:11).

- Just as one should love God,

  one should love Christ (Eph 6:24; 2 Cor 5:14).

- As one boasts in God,

  one should boast in Christ (Phil 3:3).

- Just as one should be well-pleasing to God (Rom 14:18),

  so one should be well-pleasing to Christ (2 Cor 5:9).

- As one fears God,

  one also fears Christ (Eph 5.21).

- Just as Christians serve God as slaves,

  so they serve Christ as slaves (Rom 14:18),[22] are slaves of Christ (Rom 1:1)[23] and servants of Christ (2 Cor 11:23).[24]

- Through Christ

  Paul gives thanks to God (Rom 1:8; 7:25).

- Through Jesus

  one boasts in God (Rom 5:11).

According to 1 Tim 5:21; 6:13; 2 Tim 4:1, Christians are to appear before both God and Christ.

---

20. See Eph 5:5; Col 1:13; cf. 2 Tim 4:1.

21. See also Phil 1:29; cf. 1 Tim 1:16. Paul speaks of faith in Christ in Gal 3:26; Eph 1:15; Col 1:4; 2:5; cf. 1 Tim 3:13; 2 Tim 1:13; 3:15; and probably also in Rom 3:22, 26; Gal 2:16; 3:22; Eph 3:12; Phil 3:9.

22. See also Rom 16:18; Col 3:24.

23. See also 1 Cor 7:22; Gal 1:10; Eph 6:6; Phil 1:1; Col 4:12.

24. See also Col 1:17; cf. 1 Tim 4:6. Paul speaks of Christians as servants (ὑπηρέτας) of Christ in 1 Cor 4:1.

Paul rather readily speaks of Christ in some of the same ways he speaks of God. In some ways they are functionally parallel. Paul himself does not explicate the relationship between God and Christ, but what he says is consonant with the later development of the doctrine of the Trinity, according to which Christ is of the same substance as God the Father and they are two persons in one God.

C. THE ACTION OF CHRIST (SOTERIOLOGY)

Having seen Paul's view that salvation is a free gift and how he understands the person of Christ, we come now to the heart of his understanding of salvation, namely, the action of Christ that accomplishes it. Paul describes this succinctly in 1 Cor 15:3:

> Christ died for our sins.

Compare also Gal 1:4. As we have seen, the human need for salvation can be summed up as enslavement to sin. Paul sees the death of Christ as freeing the human race from that slavery.

Paul sometimes refers to the death of Christ as salvific without mentioning the resurrection (e.g., Rom 3:23–25).[1] It seems, however, that even when it is not mentioned explicitly, the resurrection of Jesus should be understood as belonging together with his death as part of a single salvific action.[2] Thus 1 Cor 15:3 is followed immediately by a verse stating,

> he was raised from the dead.[3]

As we have seen in "The Person of Christ," Paul knows of the preexistence of Jesus. This implies incarnation, though Paul never mentions it directly. He comes closest to this when he speaks about the preexistent one's emptying himself to become human in Phil 2:7 (cf. 2 Cor 8:9).

---

1. See also Rom 5:6–9; 8:32; 14:15; 1 Cor 1:18–25; 2:2, 8; 8:11; Gal 3:1; 6:14; Eph 2:16; Phil 3:18; Col 1:20, 22; 1 Thess 5:10.

2. See V. P. Furnish, *Theology and Ethics*, 162–71; Fitzmyer, *Paul and His Theology*, 54–56; Beker, *Paul the Apostle*, 194–208; Dunn, *Theology of Paul*, 235–37.

3. Likewise Rom 5:6–9 is followed by v. 10, and 8:32 is followed by v. 34. See also Rom 14:9; 2 Cor 5:14–15; 13:4; 1 Thess 4:14. 1 Cor 11:26 speaks of the Lord's Supper as a proclamation of the Lord's death until he comes; resurrection is not explicitly mentioned but is implied by the reference to the Lord's coming after his death.

[Christ] emptied himself, taking the form of a slave, being
born in human likeness.

But just as preexistence is not central to Paul's understanding of
Jesus as Savior, so incarnation is not the saving event. Even though
Paul implicitly affirms Jesus' incarnation, Jesus, for Paul, saves by
means of his death and resurrection, not his incarnation. Of course,
if Jesus was preexistent, his incarnation was necessary in order for
him to undergo death and resurrection.

As we have seen in "Humanity apart from Christ," Paul
regards death as a consequence of sin, the principal sign of the
world's alienation from God and its enslavement to false gods. For
Paul, death is completely evil, not part of God's good creation. But
this makes it problematic that the death of Christ be part of God's
salvation of the human race. How can something evil such as death
be part of something good such as salvation? This problem is
sharpened by the kind of death Jesus suffered, that is, crucifixion, a
particularly painful and humiliating death.

Paul takes this problem seriously and argues that God's use of
Jesus' death to save the human race from sin shows that God's way
of looking at things and doing things is different from that of
human beings.[4] In 1 Cor 1:18–25 Paul argues that God's use of
Jesus' crucifixion to save the world does not make sense either to
Jews, who demand signs, or to Greeks, who desire wisdom (vv.
22–23).

> 18 For the message about the cross is foolishness to those who
> are perishing, but to us who are being saved it is the power of
> God. 19 For it is written, "I will destroy the wisdom of the
> wise, and the discernment of the discerning I will thwart."
> 20 Where is the one who is wise? Where is the scribe? Where
> is the debater of this age? Has not God made foolish the wis-
> dom of the world? 21 For since, in the wisdom of God, the
> world did not know God through wisdom, God decided,
> through the foolishness of our proclamation, to save those who
> believe. 22 For Jews demand signs and Greeks desire wisdom,
> 23 but we proclaim Christ crucified, a stumbling block to

---

4. Bornkamm, *Paul*, 158–64; Meeks, *First Urban Christians*, 180–83.

Jews and foolishness to Gentiles, 24 but to those who are the called, both Jews and Greeks, Christ the power of God and the wisdom of God. 25 For God's foolishness is wiser than human wisdom, and God's weakness is stronger than human strength.

God's foolishness and weakness in making use of Jesus' crucifixion to save the human race are wiser than human wisdom and stronger than human strength (v. 25). By means of them, God has destroyed the wisdom of the wise in accord with Isa 29:14 and Ps 33:10 (v. 19). Paul refers to the cross as a scandal in Gal 5:11. Elsewhere Paul argues that God makes the same surprising use of the foolishness and weakness of those who follow Jesus (1 Cor 4:9–13; 2 Cor 4:7–11; 12:7–10). The followers of Jesus are conformed to him in this way. As Paul says in 2 Cor 4:11,

> For while we live, we are always being given up to death for Jesus' sake, so that the life of Jesus may be made visible in our mortal flesh.

But even if we accept that, astonishingly, God has made use of the death and resurrection of Jesus to accomplish salvation, it remains to be explained how God did so. Paul offers more than one explanation, though one of them is more central than the others. The reason seems to be that faith in Jesus as Savior through his death and resurrection preceded explanation of how his death and resurrection were salvific. Just as Paul's recognition of Jesus as Savior probably preceded his understanding of the plight from which Jesus saved the human race, so it preceded his understanding of how Jesus accomplished salvation.

J. C. Beker has argued at length that within the framework of Jewish apocalyptic expectation, the resurrection of Jesus constituted the beginning of God's salvation of the world.[5] But this indicated only that Jesus' resurrection was a saving event, not precisely how it was salvific. Paul and other early Christians began by believing that Jesus was the Savior; explaining how he was the Savior followed. This means that there is no definitive explanation of how Jesus saves; both

---

5. Beker, *Paul the Apostle*, 135–81.

in the New Testament writings and subsequently, Christians have produced many different explanations of how Jesus saved the human race.[6] We will examine three explanations found in Paul.

Sacrifice

At times Paul sees the death of Jesus as a sacrifice, freeing the human race from sin by making reparation for it as the sacrifices of the Jewish cult (and other cults) did. The principal passage in which Paul speaks in these terms is Rom 3:24–26.

> 24 [All] are now justified by his grace as a gift, through the redemption that is in Christ Jesus, 25 whom God put forward as a sacrifice of atonement by his blood, effective through faith. He did this to show his righteousness, because in his divine forbearance he had passed over the sins previously committed; 26 it was to prove at the present time that he himself is righteous and that he justifies the one who has faith in Jesus.

Here Paul says that God put Christ forward "as a sacrifice of atonement by his blood" (v. 25). Compare Eph 5:2. Understanding the death of Jesus as a sacrifice may also be in view when Paul refers to the blood of Jesus as the means of being made righteous (Rom 5:9) or to a new covenant in the blood of Jesus (1 Cor 11:25).[7] And it may be in view when Paul refers to God's sending Jesus to deal with sin in Rom 8:3.

Understanding the death of Jesus as a sacrifice is clearly in view in 1 Cor 5:7, where Paul says,

> our paschal lamb, Christ, has been sacrificed.

Paul compares the death of Jesus to the slaughter of the paschal lamb. He is probably thinking that just as slaughter of the lamb at

---

6. See Callan, *Origins of Christian Faith*, 37–38.

7. See also Eph 1:7; 2:13; Col 1:20. On Paul's understanding of the death of Jesus as a sacrifice, see Bultmann, *Theology of the New Testament*, 1:295–96; Ridderbos, *Paul*, 186–90; Dunn, *Theology of Paul*, 212–25. Schoeps does not distinguish between the ideas that Jesus' death was a sacrifice and that it was vicarious (*Paul*, 128–41).

the passover and putting its blood on the doors of the Israelites' houses saved their firstborn from the angel of death (Exod 12:1–28), so the sacrifice of Jesus saved those who believe in him from sin and death.

Understanding the death of Jesus as a sacrifice is also in view in Rom 8:32. Here Paul says that God

did not withhold his own Son, but gave him up for all of us.

This language alludes to Gen 22:16–17, where God tells Abraham,

because you…have not withheld your son, your only son, I will indeed bless you.

N. A. Dahl has argued that this allusion reflects the view that the death of Jesus is a fulfillment of God's promise to Abraham that is commensurate with that on which the promise is based. God made the promise because Abraham was willing to sacrifice his son Isaac. God fulfills the promise by actually sacrificing his Son, Jesus. Thus the death of Jesus is a sacrifice, as the death of Isaac would have been if accomplished. And the sacrifice of Jesus brings the blessing God promised Abraham. In Dahl's words, the atonement is an adequate reward for the *akedah* (i.e., the binding of Isaac).[8]

Understanding Jesus' death as a sacrifice is something that might have occurred rather readily to people of the first century, since sacrifice was a central element of Judaism and all other contemporary religions. It was also an idea that fit Jesus' death rather well. Although crucifixion was not a sacrifice, it was, like sacrifice, the killing of a living being. Interpretation of Jesus' death as a sacrifice is common in the New Testament (see especially Hebrews), and it has been a popular idea in later Christian theology. Nevertheless, it is not Paul's main explanation of how Jesus' death is salvific.[9]

---

8. See Schoeps, *Paul*, 141–49; Dahl, "The Atonement: An Adequate Reward for the Akedah?" in *Jesus the Christ*, 137–51.

9. So Bultmann, *Theology of the New Testament*, 1:296; Fitzmyer, *Paul and His Theology*, 55; contra Dunn, *Theology of Paul*, 213.

One indication of this is Paul's view, discussed above, that the crucifixion of Jesus is a scandal. Understood as a sacrifice, the death of Jesus fits into a familiar category. If this were Paul's main view of Jesus' death, he would hardly speak of it as something completely alien to ordinary human understanding.

Vicarious Death

Paul also speaks in ways suggesting that he sees Jesus' death as vicarious, freeing the human race from sin by suffering in its place the punishment due sin. One passage in which we find this view is Gal 3:10–14.

> 10 For all who rely on the works of the law are under a curse; for it is written, "Cursed is everyone who does not observe and obey all the things written in the book of the law." 11 Now it is evident that no one is justified before God by the law; for "The one who is righteous will live by faith." 12 But the law does not rest on faith; on the contrary, "Whoever does the works of the law will live by them." 13 Christ redeemed us from the curse of the law by becoming a curse for us—for it is written, "Cursed is everyone who hangs on a tree"—14 in order that in Christ Jesus the blessing of Abraham might come to the Gentiles, so that we might receive the promise of the Spirit through faith.

Here Paul says that all who do not keep the law (by which he means everyone) are under a curse (v. 10). In being crucified, Christ was subject to the curse of Deut 21:23, "Cursed is everyone who hangs on a tree." Christ redeemed human beings by becoming a curse for them (v. 13), taking their curse on himself and setting them free from it. Paul also seems to see Jesus' death as vicarious in 2 Cor 5:21 and Rom 8:3.[10]

Both the understanding of Jesus' death as a sacrifice and the apparent understanding of it as vicarious can be expressed by saying that Christ died for (ὑπέρ) people. The former is clear in Rom 8:32

---

10. See Bultmann, *Theology of the New Testament*, 1:296–97; Ridderbos, *Paul*, 190–92; Dunn, *Theology of Paul*, 225–27.

and Eph 5:2, the latter in Gal 3:13 and 2 Cor 5:21. The meaning of the expression is ambiguous in Rom 5:6–8 and other passages.[11]

> 6 For while we were still weak, at the right time Christ died for the ungodly. 7 Indeed, rarely will anyone die for a righteous person—though perhaps for a good person someone might actually dare to die. 8 But God proves his love for us in that while we still were sinners Christ died for us.

It is said above that Paul *seems to see* Jesus' death as vicarious in these passages because these passages should probably be understood as expressions of Paul's third explanation of how the death and resurrection of Jesus are salvific, an explanation that is Paul's main understanding.

Union with Jesus in Death and Resurrection

Paul's most basic understanding of the way Jesus' death and resurrection save the human race from sin is that the one who believes in Jesus is united with him in his death and resurrection. Through this union, the believer dies with Jesus to the power of sin and rises with him to a new life of freedom.[12] This understanding is expressed most clearly in Rom 5:12–6:11; 7:1–4, which we will discuss below. Paul also speaks of death with Christ to sin in Col 2:11–12. Here he refers to death with Christ as a spiritual circumcision that is followed by rising with Christ.

> 11 In him also you were circumcised with a spiritual circumcision, by putting off the body of the flesh in the circumcision of

---

11. See Rom 14:15; 1 Cor 11:24–25; 2 Cor 5:14–15; Gal 2:20; Eph 5:25; Col 1:24; 1 Thess 5:10; cf. also Titus 2:14.

12. See Bultmann, *Theology of the New Testament*, 1:298–300; Robinson, *The Body*, 34–48, esp. 43–48; R. C. Tannehill, *Dying and Rising with Christ*; Furnish, *Theology and Ethics*, 171–80; Ridderbos, *Paul*, 57–68, 206–14. Sanders expresses similar ideas somewhat differently (*Paul and Palestinian Judaism*, 463–68). Dunn sees union with Christ in death as an aspect of Paul's understanding of the death of Jesus as sacrifice, although he admits that this is not known to be part of the Hebrew theology of sacrifice (*Theology of Paul*, 221–23).

Christ; 12 when you were buried with him in baptism, you
were also raised with him through faith in the power of God,
who raised him from the dead.

By dying with Christ, believers have been set free from the body of
flesh, that is, sin.[13] The same idea is restated somewhat differently
in verses 13–14. Likewise, in Gal 5:24 Paul says that those who
belong to Christ have crucified the flesh.

The idea that believers have died with Christ to sin also
underlies Paul's reference in Gal 2:19–20 to dying to the law by
being crucified with Christ.

19 For through the law I died to the law, so that I might live
to God. I have been crucified with Christ; 20 and it is no
longer I who live, but it is Christ who lives in me. And the life
I now live in the flesh I live by faith in the Son of God, who
loved me and gave himself for me.

Paul implies that crucifixion with Christ has meant Paul's death to
the law. This death has been followed by new life. Similarly, in Gal
6:14 Paul says that the cross of Christ is the means by which Paul
has been crucified to the world. In Col 2:20; 3:1–4 Paul speaks of
dying with Christ to the elemental spirits of the universe; this is followed by resurrection with Christ. In 2 Cor 5:14–15 Paul says that
because Christ died for all, all have died, that is, in union with
Christ. And Christ died for all so that those who live might no
longer live for themselves but rather for Christ, who died and was
raised for them.

As we have seen above, Paul regards Jesus' death as something
intrinsically evil; it is suffering the consequences of sin. For this
reason Paul says in 2 Cor 5:21 that God

made [Jesus] to be sin who knew no sin.

Jesus' crucifixion was entry into the sinful human condition that
issues in death, but without the turning away from God that constitutes sin. Similarly, in Phil 2:7 Paul equates Jesus' being born in

---

13. Tannehill, *Dying and Rising with Christ*, 49.

human likeness with taking the form of a slave because human beings are enslaved to sin. When Paul says that Jesus was "obedient unto death" (Phil 2:8), he may mean that he obeyed sin, which commands death. Jesus entered into the sinful human condition and accepted death as the consequence of doing so.

Seen in this context, Jesus' resurrection is a victory over death and the sin that leads to death. His resurrection is his exaltation to the right hand of God (Rom 8:34) in fulfillment of Ps 110:1 and his assumption of sovereignty over every evil power in the universe (Eph 1:20–22). Thus,

> 10 at the name of Jesus every knee should bend in heaven and on earth and under the earth 11 and every tongue proclaim that Jesus Christ is Lord. (Phil 2:10–11)[14]

Jesus' sovereignty over these powers is the reason nothing can separate Christians from the love of God in Christ (Rom 8:38–39). By dying and rising with Christ, Christians participate in his conquest of the powers of evil, his passage from death to life.

This is Paul's most encompassing explanation of how Jesus' death and resurrection is salvific. It is the only one of the three that gives a central place to the resurrection; the other two see the death of Jesus as the main salvific action. Likewise, it is the explanation that best accounts for the new life of Christians. Seeing Jesus' death as a sacrifice or as vicarious explains how it frees the human race from sin but says nothing more about the subsequent state of human beings than that they have been freed from sin. The idea that Christians die and rise with Christ not only explains how they have been freed from sin but also implies that by means of this they have entered into a new life in union with Jesus.[15] As we will see in

---

14. See also 1 Cor 3:22; 15:24–26; Col 2:10, 15.

15. This is reminiscent of the sayings of Jesus found in Mark 8:34–35/Matt 16:24–25/Luke 9:23–24 (cf. the parallel to the second verse in John 12:25) and Matt 10:38–39/Luke 14:27 and 17:33, "If any want to become my followers, let them deny themselves and take up their cross and follow me. For those who want to save their life will lose it, and those who lose their life for my sake, and for the sake of the gospel, will save it." These sayings, however, seem to envision imitation of the crucifixion of Jesus, not the participation in it envisioned by Paul.

"Humanity in Christ," the idea that Christians are united with Christ in death and resurrection is Paul's most important characterization of the new life into which believers enter through Christ.

Romans 5:12—6:11; 7:1–4

In Romans 5:12–19, by comparing him to Adam, Paul explains how Jesus Christ saves the human race.

> 12 Therefore, just as sin came into the world through one man, and death came through sin, and so death spread to all because all have sinned—13 sin was indeed in the world before the law, but sin is not reckoned when there is no law. 14 Yet death exercised dominion from Adam to Moses, even over those whose sins were not like the transgression of Adam, who is a type of the one who was to come. 15 But the free gift is not like the trespass. For if the many died through the one man's trespass, much more surely have the grace of God and the free gift in the grace of the one man, Jesus Christ, abounded for the many. 16 And the free gift is not like the effect of the one man's sin. For the judgment following one trespass brought condemnation, but the free gift following many trespasses brings justification. 17 If, because of the one man's trespass, death exercised dominion through that one, much more surely will those who receive the abundance of grace and the free gift of righteousness exercise dominion in life through the one man, Jesus Christ. 18 Therefore just as one man's trespass led to condemnation for all, so one man's act of righteousness leads to justification and life for all. 19 For just as by the one man's disobedience the many were made sinners, so by the one man's obedience the many will be made righteous.

Adam is a type of Christ (v. 14). The two are similar in that they are individuals whose actions have affected the whole human race (see vv. 12, 15, 18–19), but they have had opposite effects on the human race. The sin of Adam brought sin (vv. 12, 19), condemnation (vv. 16, 18), and death (vv. 12, 15, 17) to all; the righteous act (v. 18) or obedience (v. 19) of Christ, that is, his death and resurrection, brought righteousness (vv. 16–19) and life (vv. 17–18) to all as a free gift (vv. 15–17).

Paul expresses the same idea more briefly in 1 Cor 15:21–22. Here he says that just as death has come through a human being (Adam), so resurrection of the dead has come through a human being (Christ). "For as all die in Adam, so all will be made alive in Christ." Neither the Romans passage nor the 1 Corinthians passage explains how Adam and Christ have the effect on the human race that Paul describes. By using the phrases "in Adam" and "in Christ," 1 Cor 15:21–22 suggests that somehow the human race is united both with Adam and with Christ in such a way that what happens to each of these individuals also happens to those united with them. Romans 5:17 suggests the same thing in saying that death reigned through Adam whereas those made righteous will reign through Christ. This suggestion with respect to Christ becomes explicit in Rom 6:1–11.

In Rom 5:20–21 Paul says that the law came into the situation brought about by Adam in the human race, not to save from sin but to increase sin.

> 20 But law came in, with the result that the trespass multiplied; but where sin increased, grace abounded all the more, 21 so that, just as sin exercised dominion in death, so grace might also exercise dominion through justification leading to eternal life through Jesus Christ our Lord.

This occurred because sin reigned over all through death (v. 21). As Paul explains more fully in Romans 7, people enslaved to sin could not keep the law. Therefore the law was an occasion for the increase of sin. But the free gift of salvation surpassed sin. Through Jesus Christ this free gift reigned by making people righteous so that they might have eternal life (v. 21). God's use of the law in this way raises the possibility that Christians should continue in sin so that grace, which always surpasses it, may abound (6:1). In order to reject this suggestion, Paul further explains the Christian's relationship to sin.

In Rom 6:2–11, by saying that they have died to sin, Paul rejects the suggestion that Christians continue in sin. Clearly Paul does not mean that sin is no longer possible for Christians; in that case it would not be necessary to argue against continuing in sin. Death to sin means, however, that sin can and should be left behind definitively. In the time before the coming of Christ, God gave the law to increase sin in preparation for his coming. At that time sin had a place in God's plan of salvation. This is no longer true after the coming of Christ. The salvation offered by Christ is freedom from slavery to sin. Once we have received this freedom, it makes no sense to return to slavery.

In verses 3–5 Paul explains that Christians have died to sin by dying with Christ in baptism.

> 3 Do you not know that all of us who have been baptized into Christ Jesus were baptized into his death? 4 Therefore we have been buried with him by baptism into death, so that, just as Christ was raised from the dead by the glory of the Father, so we too might walk in newness of life. 5 For if we have been united with him in a death like his, we will certainly be united with him in a resurrection like his.

In baptism the Christian is united with Christ in such a way that he or she has undergone death and burial with Christ (vv. 3–4). Paul seems to see resurrection with Christ as still lying in the future (v. 5, cf. v. 8; 1 Cor 15:22). The Christian, however, has already entered upon a new life with Christ (v. 4). This seems to imply that in some sense the Christian has already risen with Christ although the fullness of resurrection with Christ will occur in the future.

In verses 6–7 Paul offers one way of understanding how death with Christ frees Christians from sin.

> 6 We know that our old self was crucified with him so that the body of sin might be destroyed, and we might no longer be enslaved to sin. 7 For whoever has died is freed from sin.

Paul says that the Christian's old self was crucified with Christ to end slavery to sin. The servitude of the slave comes to an end at death. The master no longer has power over the slave once the slave has died. Of course, if death is simply the end of life, it is a freedom from slavery that does the slave little good. But if the dead slave returned to life, he or she would begin a new life as a free person. Christians have died with Christ as slaves of sin and enter upon a new life of freedom with Christ.

Paul presents a somewhat different idea in verses 9–10.

> 9 We know that Christ, being raised from the dead, will never die again; death no longer has dominion over him. 10 The death he died, he died to sin, once for all; but the life he lives, he lives to God.

Here Paul says that the death of Christ is a singular event. Christ will never die again; death no longer has dominion over him. Death is the ultimate consequence of sin. One who has died has suffered all that sin can do; its power has been exhausted. In rising from the dead, Christ has passed beyond the power of sin and death. In dying with Christ and entering upon a new life, Christians have also passed beyond the power of sin and death. Even though full resurrection with Christ still lies in the future, Christians should consider themselves "dead to sin and alive to God in Christ Jesus" (v. 11).

In Rom 7:1–4 Paul offers another perspective on the effect of death with Christ on the human situation.

> 1 Do you not know, brothers and sisters—for I am speaking to those who know the law—that the law is binding on a person only during that person's lifetime? 2 Thus a married woman is bound by the law to her husband as long as he lives; but if her husband dies, she is discharged from the law concerning the husband. 3 Accordingly, she will be called an adulteress if she lives with another man while her husband is alive. But if her husband dies, she is free from that law, and if she marries another man, she is not an adulteress. 4 In the same way, my friends, you have died to the law through the body of Christ, so that you may belong to another, to him who has been raised from the dead in order that we may bear fruit for God.

Here he argues that death with Christ is death to the law, which Paul sees as closely connected with sin and death. He compares death with Christ to the situation of a woman whose husband dies. While her husband lives, she is bound by law to her husband and commits adultery if she lives with another man. But after her husband dies, she is free from that law and is not an adulteress if she lives with another man.

This illustrates well how death sets one free from the law. But it does not correspond exactly to the situation of the Christian. In this example the wife is set free from the law by the death of her husband. Paul sees Christians as set free from the law by their own death in union with Christ. Naturally, there is no analogue of this in the realm of ordinary human dealing with law.

D. SALVATION AS DEATH WITH CHRIST TO SIN

Having seen how Paul understands the saving action of Christ, we proceed to explore further the effects of that action. In doing so, we will deepen our understanding of what salvation means for Paul. We will consider the meaning of salvation from two points of view. This section discusses Christians' escape from the power of sin by dying and rising with Christ. The following section discusses the new life Christians have gained through Christ from two perspectives—present and future. Under the former we will discuss the new life into which Christians have already entered by dying and rising with Christ; under the latter we will discuss the new life that still lies in the future.

Salvation as death to sin has been in view since "Humanity apart from Christ." In that discussion we saw that Paul understands the human race as needing salvation because it is enslaved to sin. Therefore a principal result of salvation is freedom from sin. Paul states this succinctly in Rom 6:22:

You have been freed from sin.

We have previously seen that death is a consequence of sin and that the law was given to increase sin in order to prepare for the coming of salvation. Therefore freedom from sin also brings freedom from death and from the law. We will consider below Paul's extensive discussion of the relationship between sin and law in Romans 7.

Paul uses at least six different metaphors in speaking about Christians' escape from sin through Christ. Many of them we have encountered already. We will briefly discuss each of them here.

1. Freedom

The most direct and therefore most important expression of the Christian's freedom from sin is simply to say that he or she has been set free, as Paul does in Rom 6:18–22. Sin is slavery, the inability to do anything other than serve the false gods human beings have put in the place of God. Dying and rising with Christ restore the freedom humans had before they began to serve idols. Through Christ human beings once again have the freedom to choose whether or not to acknowledge God as God and themselves as creatures of God. Paul also speaks of freedom as the result of union with Christ in Gal 5:1 and elsewhere.[1]

2. Salvation

This description of Paul's theology has used "salvation" as a general term for God's deliverance of the human race through Christ. Here we observe that Paul himself does not do this. For Paul, salvation is one of several ways of referring to what results from death with Christ to sin. Salvation is closely related to freedom but has a more general meaning—rescue from evil or harm of any kind.[2] In Rom 1:16 Paul says,

[The gospel] is the power of God for salvation.

He also speaks of salvation as accomplished by Christ in Rom 10:1 and elsewhere.[3] Paul refers to Christ as Savior in Eph 5:23 and Phil 3:20.[4] He speaks of Christ as saving people in Rom 5:9–10 and elsewhere.[5]

---

1. See 2 Cor 3:17; Gal 2:4; 4:21–31; 5:13; cf. 1 Cor 9:1, 19; 10:29. Rom 8:21 speaks of freedom as a future result of dying and rising with Christ. On freedom, see Sanders, *Paul and Palestinian Judaism*, 468; Beker, *Paul the Apostle*, 269–71; Meeks, *First Urban Christians*, 184–85; Fitzmyer, *Paul and His Theology*, 67–68.

2. On salvation, see Fitzmyer, *Paul and His Theology*, 61–62; Dunn, *Theology of Paul*, 329.

3. See Rom 10:10; 11:11; 2 Cor 6:2; Eph 1:13; Phil 1:28; 2:12; 1 Thess 5:9; 2 Thess 2:13; cf. 2 Tim 2:10; 3:15.

4. Cf. also 2 Tim 1:10; Titus 1:4; 2:13; 3:6.

5. See Rom 8:24; 10:9, 13; 1 Cor 1:18; 10:33; 15:2; 2 Cor 2:15; Eph 2:5, 8; 1 Thess 2:16; 2 Thess 2:10; cf. 1 Tim 1:15.

3. Redemption

Redemption is another closely related way of talking about release from the power of sin.[6] Redemption refers to setting a slave or a captive free by purchase or payment of ransom. In Rom 3:24 Paul says,

> Redemption...is in Christ Jesus.

He also speaks of redemption through Christ in 1 Cor 1:30 and elsewhere.[7] Paul expresses the same idea by saying in 1 Cor 6:20 that Christians were bought for a price.[8]

4. Sanctification

In the Hebrew Bible, God is said to be holy because God is unlike anything else that exists.[9] People and things are said to be holy insofar as they are associated with God; thus the Spirit of God is the Holy Spirit. This association with God can be understood in a cultic sense as separation from profane people, places, and things or in an ethical sense as separation from social and individual wrongdoing.

Idolatry is the opposite of association with God; the consequent enslavement to sin makes one permanently unholy by preventing one from turning back to God. Conversely, release from enslavement to sin makes people holy by restoring their association with God.[10] It is release from everything that prevents one's association with God.

In 1 Cor 1:30, using "sanctification" as synonymous with "redemption" (see also 2 Thess 2:13), Paul says that Christ is the sanctification of Christians.

---

6. On redemption, see Ridderbos, *Paul*, 193–97; Fitzmyer, *Paul and His Theology*, 66–67; Dunn, *Theology of Paul*, 227–28, 328.

7. See Eph 1:7; Col 1:14; cf. 1 Tim 2:6; Titus 2:14. In Rom 8:23 redemption of the body is said to lie in the future; cf. also Eph 1:14; 4:30. Cf. the saying of Jesus found in Mark 10:45/Matt 20:28, "For the Son of Man came not to be served but to serve, and to give his life a ransom for many."

8. See also 1 Cor 7:23; Gal 3:13; 4:5.

9. On holiness in the Hebrew Bible, see J. G. Gammie, *Holiness in Israel*.

10. On sanctification, see Ridderbos, *Paul*, 260–65; Fitzmyer, *Paul and His Theology*, 68–69; Dunn, *Theology of Paul*, 330.

Christ Jesus…became for us…righteousness and sanctification
and redemption.

In Rom 15:16 and elsewhere, Paul refers to Christians as ones who
have been sanctified.[11] He frequently refers to Christians as holy.
In the salutations of his letters, Paul often refers to those he
addresses as called to be holy ones (Rom 1:7; 1 Cor 1:2) or simply
as holy ones.[12] He also refers to them as holy ones at other points
in his letters.[13]

In addition to speaking about sanctification as an accomplished reality, Paul also speaks of it as needing to be attained. In
1 Thess 4:3 Paul says that the will of God is the sanctification of
people, introducing an argument for a certain kind of behavior (see
vv. 4 and 7); he says similar things elsewhere.[14]

5. Reconciliation

To speak of reconciliation as accomplished by Christ implies
that sin is a disruption of the human race's relationship with God.
In turning from the true God to worship false gods, human beings
have abandoned their proper relationship with God, who created
them. Dying and rising with Christ overcome the resulting
enslavement to false gods and restore the right relationship with
God.[15] Paul refers to reconciliation of the human race to God
through the death of Christ in Rom 5:10–11, which says in part:

---

11. See 1 Cor 1:2; 6:11; Eph 5:26, 27. In 1 Cor 7:14 Paul says that non-Christians
who are married to Christians are sanctified by their relationship to the Christian
spouse and thus their children are holy.

12. See 2 Cor 1:1; Eph 1:1; Phil 1:1; Col 1:2.

13. See Rom 8:27; 12:13; 15:25–26, 31; 16:2, 15; 1 Cor 6:1–2; 14:33; 16:1, 15; 2
Cor 8:4; 9:1, 12; Eph 1:4, 15, 18; 2:19; 3:8, 18; 4:12; 5:3; 6:18; Phil 4:21–22; Col 1:4,
12, 22, 26; 3:12; 2 Thess 1:10; Phlm 5, 7; cf. 1 Tim 5:10.

14. See Rom 6:19, 22; 12:1; 1 Cor 7:34. In 1 Thess 5:23 Paul prays that God will
sanctify his addressees; in 3:13 he prays that God will strengthen them in holiness.

15. On reconciliation, see Bultmann, *Theology of the New Testament*, 1:285–87;
Ridderbos, *Paul*, 182–86; Sanders, *Paul and Palestinian Judaism*, 469–70; Meeks, *First
Urban Christians*, 186–87; Fitzmyer, *Paul and His Theology*, 62–63; Dunn, *Theology of
Paul*, 228–30, 328.

We were reconciled to God through the death of his Son.

In Rom 11:15 Paul says that the unbelief of some Jews has contributed to the reconciliation of the world. And in 2 Cor 5:18–20 Paul makes it clear that God brought about reconciliation between himself and the human race through Christ.[16]

6. Being Made Righteous

Paul often refers to release from sin through Christ by speaking of Christians' being made righteous.[17] Humanity's enslavement to sin results in transgression of the law, which is the opposite of righteousness. By dying and rising with Christ, human beings are set free from the power of sin and cease to transgress the law. In this way they are made righteous.

Speaking about Christ as making human beings righteous should probably be understood as a forensic metaphor. Human beings are envisioned as standing before a judge; by the action of Christ, they are found to be righteous, that is, not deserving of punishment. It is not entirely clear whether Paul thinks they are found to be righteous because they have been made intrinsically righteous or because they have been declared righteous, that is, received a pardon. In either case, their righteousness qualifies them for life and is thus equivalent to life.

This way of speaking about release from sin is especially common in Romans and Galatians, where Paul argues that Gentile Christians should not keep the Jewish law. Against the argument that keeping the law would lead to righteousness, Paul argues that dying and rising with Christ makes Christians righteous as a free gift, apart from the law. In "Salvation as a Free Gift," we examined Paul's argument for this point in Rom 3:21–4:25. We find other

---

16. Cf. also Col 1:20, 22. Paul also speaks of reconciliation in Eph 2:16.

17. On being made righteous, see Bultmann, *Theology of the New Testament*, 1:270–85; Ridderbos, *Paul*, 161–78; Sanders, *Paul and Palestinian Judaism*, 470–72; Beker, *Paul the Apostle*, 260–64; Meeks, *First Urban Christians*, 185–86; Fitzmyer, *Paul and His Theology*, 59–61; Dunn, *Theology of Paul*, 334–89.

references to righteousness as the result of dying with Christ in Rom 5:1 and elsewhere, including 1 Cor 1:30, cited above.[18]

Paul makes such extensive use of language about being made righteous that many have seen this as the central theme of his thought. In the last century this has often been challenged.[19] In agreement with these challenges, I do not regard this language as central to Paul's thinking. We have seen in "The Action of Christ" that union with Christ in death and resurrection is the central element of Paul's soteriology. We will see in "Humanity in Christ" that it is also central to Paul's understanding of the new life into which Christians enter through Christ.

Romans 7

In this passage Paul argues that dying and rising with Christ set Gentile Christians free from the law. This does not mean, however, that the law itself is evil. In "The Action of Christ," we have already seen that Rom 7:1–4 provides an illustration of how death sets one free from the law: the death of a spouse sets one free from the law binding one to the spouse. In vv. 4–6 Paul shows how this example applies to dying with Christ and so being set free from the law.

> 4 In the same way, my friends, you have died to the law through the body of Christ, so that you may belong to another, to him who has been raised from the dead in order that we may bear fruit for God. 5 While we were living in the flesh, our sinful passions, aroused by the law, were at work in our members to bear fruit for death. 6 But now we are discharged from the law, dead to that which held us captive, so that we are slaves not under the old written code but in the new life of the Spirit.

---

18. See Rom 5:9, 17, 19; 6:7; 8:30, 33; 9:30; 10:4, 6, 10; 1 Cor 1:30 (where being made righteous is synonymous with redemption and sanctification); 6:11; 2 Cor 3:9; 5:21; 6:14; Gal 2:16–17, 21; 3:6, 8, 24; 5:4–5; Phil 1:11; 3:9; cf. Titus 3:7.

19. For a recent discussion of this history of interpretation, see S. Westerholm, *Perspectives Old and New on Paul*. Bornkamm is one of those who argue that being made righteous is central to Paul's thought (*Paul*, 115–17, 154–56).

In verse 4 Paul says that Christians have died to the law through the body of Christ. By becoming part of the body of Christ, Christians participate in the death and resurrection of Jesus. Just as Jesus' death and resurrection set him free from sin and death, so Christians' union with him in death and resurrection sets them free from sin and death (see Rom 6:6–11). It also sets them free from the law because the law was given to increase sin (Rom 7:5) so that people would be ready to accept salvation when it was offered through Christ. The coming of salvation also means freedom from the law (v. 6) because the purpose of the law has been fulfilled.

In verse 5 Paul says that Christians are no longer living in the flesh. As we saw in "Humanity apart from Christ," Paul does not use "flesh" literally here. Rather, "flesh" indicates the situation of alienation from God though idolatry and consequent enslavement to sin and death. Those who have been set free from sin, death, and law are no longer in the "flesh."

Having briefly indicated that dying and rising with Christ sets one free from the law as well as from sin and death, Paul goes on to argue that this does not mean the law in itself is something bad. Rather, the law is good but became part of the way sin dominated human beings for God's good purposes. In making this argument, Paul also explains exactly how the law was associated with sin.

> 7 What then should we say? That the law is sin? By no means! Yet, if it had not been for the law, I would not have known sin. I would not have known what it is to covet if the law had not said, "You shall not covet." 8 But sin, seizing an opportunity in the commandment, produced in me all kinds of covetousness. Apart from the law sin lies dead. 9 I was once alive apart from the law, but when the commandment came, sin revived 10 and I died, and the very commandment that promised life proved to be death to me. 11 For sin, seizing an opportunity in the commandment, deceived me and through it killed me. 12 So the law is holy, and the commandment is holy and just and good.

In verse 7 Paul asks if the law is sin and rejects this possibility emphatically. The law, however, was the means by which people became conscious of sin. Paul implies that even though sin dominated human beings before the giving of the law, in some way it was quiescent (vv. 8b–9). When the law was given, sin came to life (v. 9) and multiplied, leading to death (v. 11). As an example, Paul uses the commandment "You shall not covet." Sin made use of this commandment to increase covetousness (vv. 7–8). Giving a commandment to people under the power of sin does not make it possible for them to keep it. Instead the commandment becomes the occasion for increased activity contrary to it. In this way a commandment good in itself (v. 12) becomes part of the enslavement of human beings to sin and death. Paul presumes that this was God's intention in giving the law.

Paul then goes on to make the same point somewhat differently in verses 13–20 and 21–25.

> 13 Did what is good, then, bring death to me? By no means! It was sin, working death in me through what is good, in order that sin might be shown to be sin, and through the commandment might become sinful beyond measure. 14 For we know that the law is spiritual; but I am of the flesh, sold into slavery under sin. 15 I do not understand my own actions. For I do not do what I want, but I do the very thing I hate. 16 Now if I do what I do not want, I agree that the law is good. 17 But in fact it is no longer I that do it, but sin that dwells within me. 18 For I know that nothing good dwells within me, that is, in my flesh. I can will what is right, but I cannot do it. 19 For I do not do the good I want, but the evil I do not want is what I do. 20 Now if I do what I do not want, it is no longer I that do it, but sin that dwells within me.

In verse 13 Paul asks if the good law brought death to human beings, and again he rejects this idea emphatically. It was not the law, but sin making use of the law, that brought death. And the purpose of this was to bring sin to light and to make it sinful beyond measure, as a preparation for the gift of salvation. We can see that the law is good because human beings agree with the law and want to do what it commands (v. 16). But they find themselves unable to do what they want (vv. 15–20) because the power of sin at work in them prevents it (vv. 17, 20).

21 So I find it to be a law that when I want to do what is good, evil lies close at hand. 22 For I delight in the law of God in my inmost self, 23 but I see in my members another law at war with the law of my mind, making me captive to the law of sin that dwells in my members. 24 Wretched man that I am! Who will rescue me from this body of death? 25 Thanks be to God through Jesus Christ our Lord! So then, with my mind I am a slave to the law of God, but with my flesh I am a slave to the law of sin.

In verse 22 Paul says that he delights in the law of God in his inner self, thus showing that the law of God is good. But he sees in his members another law at war with the law of his mind, making him captive to the law of sin that dwells in his members (v. 23). This other law, the law of sin, is the power of sin that enslaves people apart from Christ. Through Christ, however, God has saved people from this body of death (vv. 24 25).

E. SALVATION AS NEW LIFE WITH CHRIST

As we have already noted, Paul sees dying and rising with Christ not only as freedom from sin but also as the beginning of new life. This new life is twofold—Christians already experience it partly in the present, but they will experience it completely in the future. Paul's most important way of speaking about new life with Christ is to speak about the union of Christians with Christ. We will discuss this in "Humanity in Christ." Here we will consider some of the other ways Paul presents new life with Christ.

Already

The principal way that Christians already experience new life with Christ is summed up in Rom 8:14:

All who are led by the Spirit of God are children of God.

Christians' possession of the Spirit of God is the main way they presently experience new life with Christ.[1] The Spirit is the blessing that comes to humanity through Christ (Gal 3:14). It is the pledge, God's down payment on salvation (2 Cor 1:22; 5:5; Eph 1:14).

We have seen above (in discussing Paul's view of God) that Paul takes over from the Hebrew scriptures the view that God possesses a Spirit, and the understanding of it as analogous to the spirit of human beings. In discussing Paul's anthropology, we have seen that Paul understands the human spirit as the aspect of the human being that knows and wills. Thus the Spirit of God is God insofar

---

1. On the Spirit, see Schweitzer, *Mysticism of Paul,* 160–76; Bornkamm, *Paul,* 180–82; Ridderbos, *Paul,* 214–23; Beker, *Paul the Apostle,* 278–86; Fitzmyer, "Pauline Teaching," 124–26; Dunn, *Theology of Paul,* 413–41. R. Bultmann understands Paul's view of the Spirit as something taken over from the kerygma of the Hellenistic church (*Theology of the New Testament,* 1:153–64).

as God knows and wills, the active aspect of God, who, unlike humans, has no passive aspect.

In "The Person of Christ," we have seen that Christ shares the Spirit of God. One way of expressing the unity of Christ with God is to say that they have the same Spirit, that they know and will in the same way.

Thus Christians' possession of the Spirit of God is a matter of being united with Christ and with God in such a way that all know and will in the same way. The active (and only) aspect of God is the active aspect of Christ and the Christian. Basically, possession of the Spirit of God is another facet of the union of Christians with Christ that we have earlier discussed in "The Action of Christ" and will discuss in "Humanity in Christ." Christians are united with Christ in such a way that what is true of him is also true of them. As Christ died and rose, so Christians die and rise with him. As Christ possesses the Spirit of God, so do Christians.

Possession of the Spirit of God, however, is a matter not only of union with Christ but also of union with God. Seen in this way, dying and rising with Christ not only free human beings from sin but also give them a share in God's life. Paul's understanding of the Spirit of God is similar to the later theological concept of sanctifying grace. Both are a matter of sharing the life of God.

Possession of the Spirit of God is clearly something that Christians experience personally. When Paul asks the Galatians,

> Did you receive the Spirit by doing the works of the law or by believing what you heard? (Gal 3:2),

he presupposes that they experienced their reception of the Spirit in circumstances they can identify without any ambiguity. One thing that might underlie this is what the Acts of the Apostles says happened to Cornelius and his household. While Peter was preaching the gospel to them, the Holy Spirit fell upon them, and they began to speak in tongues and praise God (Acts 10:44–46). Something like this may have happened to the Galatians when they heard and believed Paul's preaching. First Corinthians 12–14 makes it clear that Paul presumes many Christians speak in tongues (including himself, 14:18) and experience other extraordinary manifestations of the Spirit, including prophecy.

Paul also speaks of experiencing the Spirit of God in prayer. In Gal 4:6 he says that God has sent the Spirit of his Son into the hearts of Christians, crying "Abba! Father!" Paul says the same thing in Rom 8:15. Later he says that when Christians do not know how to pray, the Spirit "intercedes with sighs too deep for words" (Rom 8:26).

Paul occasionally indicates in other ways that Christians presently experience new life with Christ.[2] Paul says that those who are in Christ are a new creation (2 Cor 5:17; Gal 6:15). He also states that they are being transformed into the glory of Christ (2 Cor 3:18; 4:6) and that Christians have been glorified (Rom 8:30). As we will see below, Paul also speaks of transformation and glory as still lying in the future.

Not Yet

Even though Christians already possess the Spirit of God, they remain lacking in some ways. This lack is summed up in Rom 8:19:

Creation waits with eager longing for the revealing of the children of God.

Christians are already children of God but not yet revealed as children of God. Christians are children of God who have been conceived and have developed in the uterus but have not yet been born (see Rom 8:22). Thus the present is a time in which the children of God are coming to birth. J. C. Beker, who argues that Paul's thought is thoroughly apocalyptic, has especially emphasized the future fullness of new life with Christ.[3]

In 1 Cor 15:24–28 Paul interprets the present time as one in which Christ is progressively subjecting to himself all the powers of the universe.

---

2. On these see Meeks, *First Urban Christians*, 187–89; Fitzmyer, *Paul and His Theology*, 69–71.

3. Beker, *Paul the Apostle*. See also Meeks, *First Urban Christians*, 171–80.

24 Then comes the end, when he hands over the kingdom to God the Father, after he has destroyed every ruler and every authority and power. 25 For he must reign until he has put all his enemies under his feet. 26 The last enemy to be destroyed is death. 27 For "God has put all things in subjection under his feet." But when it says, "All things are put in subjection," it is plain that this does not include the one who put all things in subjection under him. 28 When all things are subjected to him, then the Son himself will also be subjected to the one who put all things in subjection under him, so that God may be all in all.

Christ has already risen and entered upon his reign. But he has not yet destroyed every ruler and authority and power. The last enemy to be destroyed is death. Only after Christ has done this will salvation be fully accomplished. Paul here supposes that the death and resurrection of Jesus have been a decisive moment, inaugurating the reign of Christ. Still, it is necessary to make that reign fully effective. This is what is occurring now.

Christians live partly in the new age that has already begun to appear and partly in the old age that has not yet completely ended. They need to be aware that they themselves have not arrived at the fullness of salvation, and they need to beware lest the old age determine their thought and action rather than the new age that has dawned. Paul emphasizes these points in his letters to the Corinthians. One passage in which he warns the Corinthians against being influenced excessively by the old age is 1 Cor 3:18–20.

18 Do not deceive yourselves. If you think that you are wise in this age, you should become fools so that you may become wise. 19 For the wisdom of this world is foolishness with God. For it is written, "He catches the wise in their craftiness," 20 and again, "The Lord knows the thoughts of the wise, that they are futile."

Making the point that the Corinthians have not yet reached the fullness of salvation, Paul says sarcastically in 1 Cor 4:8,

Already you have all you want! Already you have become rich! Quite apart from us you have become kings! Indeed, I wish that you had become kings, so that we might be kings with you!

The Corinthians tend to regard themselves as having come to the fullness of salvation. Paul urges them to think otherwise.

Paul can speak of future new life with Christ rather generally. In 1 Cor 13:8–13 Paul contrasts the present and future states of Christians.

> 8 Love never ends. But as for prophecies, they will come to an end; as for tongues, they will cease; as for knowledge, it will come to an end. 9 For we know only in part, and we prophesy only in part; 10 but when the complete comes, the partial will come to an end. 11 When I was a child, I spoke like a child, I thought like a child, I reasoned like a child; when I became an adult, I put an end to childish ways. 12 For now we see in a mirror, dimly, but then we will see face to face. Now I know only in part; then I will know fully, even as I have been fully known. 13 And now faith, hope, and love abide, these three; and the greatest of these is love.

He compares the present state to childhood and the future state to adulthood, the present to seeing in a mirror and the future to seeing face to face. In their present state, Christians prophesy, speak in tongues, and have knowledge. But these are partial and will come to an end. What will last into the future are faith, hope, and love, and most of all love. Paul also speaks of future new life with Christ generally in Rom 8:18–39; we will discuss this passage below.

Elsewhere Paul makes it clear that the future fullness of new life with Christ occurs at the second coming of Jesus.[4] This is discussed at some length in 1 and 2 Thessalonians and more briefly elsewhere.[5] According to 1 Thessalonians, the day of the Lord will come like a thief in the night (5:2). According to 2 Thessalonians,

---

4. On the second coming of Jesus and related matters, see Schoeps, *Paul*, 97–110; Bornkamm, *Paul*, 219–26; Ridderbos, *Paul*, 487–562; Conzelmann, *Outline*, 184–91; Dunn, *Theology of Paul*, 294–315.

5. The most extensive discussions are in 1 Thess 4:13–5:11 and 2 Thess 1:7–10; 2:1–12. It is also mentioned in 1 Thess 1:10; 2:19; 3:13; 5:23; 1 Cor 1:7–8; 11:26; 16:22; Rom 11:26; Col 3:3–4.

Christ will not come again until the rebellion takes place and the lawless one is revealed (2:3). The mystery of lawlessness is already at work but is presently being restrained (2:6–7). After the restraint is removed, Christ will come again and will destroy the lawless one with the breath of his mouth (2:8). He will also destroy those who have afflicted Christians (1:7–9; cf. 2:12). In Rom 16:20 Paul says that God will crush Satan under the feet of the Roman Christians, perhaps referring to the same event.

The destruction of evildoers at the second coming of Christ may constitute the judgment Paul mentions. As we have seen above in discussing Paul's views of God and in "The Person of Christ," Paul frequently speaks of God as judging the world and sometimes says that this judgment occurs through Christ (Rom 2:16) or that Christ judges (1 Cor 4:5; 2 Cor 5:10). Paul does not describe the final judgment, but we may assume that it takes the form of destroying the wicked at Christ's second coming.

When Christ comes again, the dead will rise (1 Thess 4:16; 1 Cor 15:22–23, 52). They will rise in a new form that Paul describes in 1 Cor 15:35–49.

> 35 But someone will ask, "How are the dead raised? With what kind of body do they come?" 36 Fool! What you sow does not come to life unless it dies. 37 And as for what you sow, you do not sow the body that is to be, but a bare seed, perhaps of wheat or of some other grain. 38 But God gives it a body as he has chosen, and to each kind of seed its own body….42 So it is with the resurrection of the dead. What is sown is perishable, what is raised is imperishable. 43 It is sown in dishonor, it is raised in glory. It is sown in weakness, it is raised in power. 44 It is sown a physical body, it is raised a spiritual body. If there is a physical body, there is also a spiritual body.

The resurrection body is like the plant that grows from a seed, whereas the ordinary body is like the seed (vv. 36–38). The ordinary body is sown perishable, dishonorable, weak, physical; it is raised imperishable, glorious, powerful, spiritual (vv. 42–44). Although Paul speaks of the final resurrection of all in 1 Cor 15:22, in the other passages mentioned above he does not seem to have anyone in view apart from those who die in Christ. He does not explicitly advert to the fate of non-Christians who have died.

Christians alive at the coming of Christ will undergo the same transformation as those raised from the dead. Paul describes this transformation in 1 Cor 15:51–54 (cf. 2 Cor 5:1–4; Phil 3:20–21).

> 51 Listen, I will tell you a mystery! We will not all die, but we will all be changed, 52 in a moment, in the twinkling of an eye, at the last trumpet. For the trumpet will sound, and the dead will be raised imperishable, and we will be changed. 53 For this perishable body must put on imperishability, and this mortal body must put on immortality. 54 When this perishable body puts on imperishability, and this mortal body puts on immortality, then the saying that is written will be fulfilled: "Death has been swallowed up in victory."

The perishable, mortal bodies of Christians will put on imperishability and immortality. When the dead rise transformed and the living are transformed, death, the final enemy, will have been conquered (1 Cor 15:26, 54–55).

In Romans 9–11, as we will see below, Paul says that in the end all of Israel will be saved. This also seems to happen at the second coming of Christ (see Rom 11:26).

In 1 Cor 15:24–28 Paul says that after all things, including death (v. 26), are subjected to Christ, then Christ will hand over the kingdom to God the Father (v. 24) so that God may be all in all (v. 28).

Romans 8

In the first half of Romans 8 (vv. 1–17), Paul speaks about the new life with Christ that Christians already experience, principally possession of the Holy Spirit; in the remainder of the chapter he speaks about the new life they do not yet experience.

> 1 There is therefore now no condemnation for those who are in Christ Jesus. 2 For the law of the Spirit of life in Christ Jesus has set you free from the law of sin and of death. 3 For God has done what the law, weakened by the flesh, could not do: by

sending his own Son in the likeness of sinful flesh, and to deal with sin, he condemned sin in the flesh, 4 so that the just requirement of the law might be fulfilled in us, who walk not according to the flesh but according to the Spirit.

In verse 2 Paul says that the law of the Spirit of life in Christ Jesus has set Christians free from the law of sin and death. Paul had ended Romans 7 by speaking of human enslavement to sin as a matter of their having within them a "law" of sin that prevents them from keeping the law of God. This law of sin leads to death. Thus, in verse 2 Paul is saying that the Spirit of life set humanity free from enslavement to sin. Paul speaks of the "law" of the Spirit of life to suggest that the Spirit is a power within the Christian that is comparable to the power of sin but opposite in its effect. The power of sin prevents humans from doing God's will; the power of the Spirit makes it possible for them to do so.

In verse 3 Paul briefly explains how Christians have come to possess the Spirit. The law God gave Israel could not save Israel from sin because Israel was weakened by the flesh. That is, the law, given to people under the power of sin, brought them no power to keep it, as Paul has argued at some length in Romans 7. So God sent his Son, Jesus, in the likeness of sinful flesh and condemned sin in his flesh, perhaps using the crucifixion of Jesus as a sin-offering. This, Paul presumes, is what gives Christians the Spirit. What underlies this is the idea we discussed in "The Action of Christ." Those who believe in Christ are united with him in death and resurrection. In Christ they experience death to the flesh, that is, to sin and death, and entry into new life. This new life is possession of the Spirit of Christ, which is also the Spirit of God.

In verse 4 Paul says that possession of the Spirit allows Christians to keep the law of God. The law of God sets forth God's will. It is not problematic because of its content but because it was incapable of setting people free from the power of sin. Once people have been set free from the power of sin, however, they do not follow the law because its purpose was to prepare for the coming of Christ, not serve as a guide for life afterwards. Instead Christians walk according to the Spirit. In this way they do the will of God, which is also what the law presents. Paul goes on to contrast walking according to the flesh and walking according to the Spirit in verses 5–8.

> 9 But you are not in the flesh; you are in the Spirit, since the Spirit of God dwells in you. Anyone who does not have the Spirit of Christ does not belong to him. 10 But if Christ is in you, though the body is dead because of sin, the Spirit is life because of righteousness. 11 If the Spirit of him who raised Jesus from the dead dwells in you, he who raised Christ from the dead will give life to your mortal bodies also through his Spirit that dwells in you.

In verse 9 Paul says that anyone who does not have the spirit of Christ, which is also the spirit of God, does not belong to Christ. This is because union with Christ is a matter of sharing everything that is Christ's – body, soul, spirit, mind, heart. If one lacks any of these, including the spirit of Christ, one is not truly united with Christ and does not belong to Christ. In verse 11 Paul says that Christians' present possession of the Spirit is their assurance that God will give life to their mortal bodies in the future.

> 14 For all who are led by the Spirit of God are children of God. 15 For you did not receive a spirit of slavery to fall back into fear, but you have received a spirit of adoption. When we cry, "Abba! Father!" 16 it is that very Spirit bearing witness with our spirit that we are children of God, 17 and if children, then heirs, heirs of God and joint heirs with Christ—if, in fact, we suffer with him so that we may also be glorified with him.

In verse 14, as we have seen, Paul says that those who are led by the Spirit of God are children of God. The underlying idea here is that sharing the Spirit of God, which is also the Spirit of Christ, is an aspect of union with Christ. And union with Christ means being what Christ is. Since Christ is Son of God, those united with Christ are also the Son of God, or, in the plural, children of God. In verses 15–16 Paul refers to the Christian cry of "Abba! Father" as showing that the presence of the Spirit within Christians makes them children of God.

In verses 18–25 Paul contrasts the present situation of Christians with their future situation.

> 18 I consider that the sufferings of this present time are not worth comparing with the glory about to be revealed to us. 19 For the creation waits with eager longing for the revealing of the children of God; 20 for the creation was subjected to futility, not of its own will but by the will of the one who subjected it, in hope 21 that the creation itself will be set free from its bondage to decay and will obtain the freedom of the glory of the children of God. 22 We know that the whole creation has been groaning in labor pains until now; 23 and not only the creation, but we ourselves, who have the first fruits of the Spirit, groan inwardly while we wait for adoption, the redemption of our bodies.

The present is a time of suffering; in the future, glory will be revealed (v. 18). Christians are already children of God but not yet revealed as such. All of creation awaits the revelation of the children of God (v. 19) because, as a result of sin, creation itself was subjected to futility and put in bondage to decay (vv. 20–21). The present is a time of suffering because creation is in labor, giving birth to the children of God (v. 22). Paul pictures the universe as a woman who has conceived children and is now giving birth to them. This captures the relationship between present and future. The children have already been conceived and have come to term, but they have not yet been born. Bringing them to birth entails labor and suffering.

This image might suggest that while the universe awaits the revelation of the children of God, Christians are already complete as children of God. In verse 23 Paul says that Christians share in the present suffering of the universe. They already have the Spirit, but this is only the firstfruits of the Christ event. They still await the completion of their adoption by God, which will be the redemption of their bodies. They hope for the future (vv. 24–25) with the help of the Spirit (vv. 26–27).

In verses 28–39 Paul argues that Christians' hope for the future is secure because of what God has already done for them.

28 We know that all things work together for good for those
who love God, who are called according to his purpose. 29 For
those whom he foreknew he also predestined to be conformed
to the image of his Son, in order that he might be the firstborn
within a large family. 30 And those whom he predestined he
also called; and those whom he called he also justified; and
those whom he justified he also glorified. 31 What then are we
to say about these things? If God is for us, who is against us?
32 He who did not withhold his own Son, but gave him up for
all of us, will he not with him also give us everything else? 33
Who will bring any charge against God's elect? It is God who
justifies. 34 Who is to condemn? It is Christ Jesus, who died,
yes, who was raised, who is at the right hand of God, who
indeed intercedes for us....38 For I am convinced that neither
death, nor life, nor angels, nor rulers, nor things present, nor
things to come, nor powers, 39 nor height, nor depth, nor anything else in all creation, will be able to separate us from the
love of God in Christ Jesus our Lord.

Christians' hope for the future is the hope that all things will
work together for the good for those who love God (v. 28), that
God will give Christians everything (v. 32), that they will not be
condemned (vv. 33–34), and that nothing will separate them from
the love of God in Christ Jesus (v. 39). This hope is based on God's
foreknowing them, predestining them to be conformed to the
image of his Son, calling them, making them righteous, and glorifying them (vv. 29–30). It is based on God's giving up his Son for
them (v. 32), on the absence of anyone to condemn them (vv.
33–34), and on the inability of anything to separate Christians from
the love of Christ, which is the love of God in Christ (vv. 35–39).

Romans 9–11

In Romans 9–11 Paul discusses one specific aspect of future
new life with Christ, namely, the fate of Israel.[6] This is problematic
because many Jews did not accept Jesus as the Messiah promised to

6. On this passage, see Schoeps, *Paul*, 235–45; Conzelmann, *Outline*, 248–54.

them by God. In Rom 9:1–5 Paul expresses his anguish over the people of Israel.

> 1 I am speaking the truth in Christ—I am not lying; my conscience confirms it by the Holy Spirit—2 I have great sorrow and unceasing anguish in my heart. 3 For I could wish that I myself were accursed and cut off from Christ for the sake of my own people, my kindred according to the flesh. 4 They are Israelites, and to them belong the adoption, the glory, the covenants, the giving of the law, the worship, and the promises; 5 to them belong the patriarchs, and from them, according to the flesh, comes the Messiah, who is over all, God blessed forever. Amen.

He would be willing to be cut off from Christ himself for their sake because they are his own people (v. 3). In verses 4–5 Paul lists the many blessings they have received from God.

The unbelief of Israel is a problem because it seems to mean that God's word to them, that is, God's promise to save them, has failed. The thesis Paul argues in this section is that the word of God has not failed, as he says in verse 6. Paul's argument for this thesis is long and complex. He develops one line of argument in 9:6–10:21 but then rejects it and offers another argument in chapter 11. This is his final position on the question.

Paul's first line of argument is that God's promise is not necessarily given to all who belong to Israel by birth; rather God could choose only some of them to be recipients of the promise. Thus the Jews that did not believe in Christ might have been rejected by God. Their unbelief would then be part of the way God fulfilled the promise to save Israel, not a failure to fulfill it.

Paul argues for this possibility by referring to events in Israel's early history. Abraham had two sons by two different women, Ishmael and Isaac, but only Isaac was the recipient of the promise of salvation (vv. 6–9).

> 6 It is not as though the word of God had failed. For not all Israelites truly belong to Israel, 7 and not all of Abraham's children are his true descendants; but "It is through Isaac that descendants shall be named for you." 8 This means that it is

not the children of the flesh who are the children of God, but the children of the promise are counted as descendants. 9 For this is what the promise said, "About this time I will return and Sarah shall have a son."

Even more strikingly, Isaac and Rebecca had two sons, Esau and Jacob, but only Jacob was the Israel who received the promise of salvation (vv. 10–13).

> 10 Nor is that all; something similar happened to Rebecca when she had conceived children by one husband, our ancestor Isaac. 11 Even before they had been born or had done anything good or bad (so that God's purpose of election might continue, 12 not by works but by his call) she was told, "The elder shall serve the younger." 13 As it is written, "I have loved Jacob, but I have hated Esau."

In the past God has chosen some Israelites by birth and rejected others, and God could be doing the same thing in the present.

This raises the possibility that God is unrighteous in making such choices (vv. 14–18).

> 14 What then are we to say? Is there injustice on God's part? By no means! 15 For he says to Moses, "I will have mercy on whom I have mercy, and I will have compassion on whom I have compassion." 16 So it depends not on human will or exertion, but on God who shows mercy. 17 For the scripture says to Pharaoh, "I have raised you up for the very purpose of showing my power in you, so that my name may be proclaimed in all the earth." 18 So then he has mercy on whomever he chooses, and he hardens the heart of whomever he chooses.

Paul seems to present two ways of seeing that God is not unrighteous. First, Paul says that such choices are a matter of God's mercy (vv. 14–16). What Paul may presuppose here is that because of its rejection of God, the human race deserves only God's punishment. If God gives mercy to some, this is not unjust because mercy is not owed to anyone. Paul's second perspective, offered in verses 17–18, is that God's failure to give mercy serves a good purpose. For example, God's hardening the heart of Pharaoh was so that God's power would be shown in him and God's name be proclaimed everywhere.

This idea that the fate of humans is entirely the result of God's granting or withholding mercy seems to imply that God cannot then find fault with those to whom he does not grant mercy (vv. 19–21).

> 19 You will say to me then, "Why then does he still find fault? For who can resist his will?" 20 But who indeed are you, a human being, to argue with God? Will what is molded say to the one who molds it, "Why have you made me like this?" 21 Has the potter no right over the clay, to make out of the same lump one object for special use and another for ordinary use?

As we have seen in "Humanity apart from Christ," Paul presumes that all must take responsibility for sin. Paul, however, does not mention this here. Instead he says that human beings are in no position to question God. They can no more call God into question than pots can call the potter into question.

Having reached this point in his argument, Paul sketches out the possibility that God could have made two sets of pots, one intended for wrath and the other for mercy, and that the latter includes both Jews and Gentiles (vv. 22–29). This would mean that Gentiles who did not seek righteousness attained it and some Jews who did seek righteousness did not attain it (vv. 30–31). How could this be? Those Jews misunderstood the way to righteousness, thinking it was based on works rather than faith (vv. 32–34). In chapter 10 Paul discusses at length this misunderstanding of the source of righteousness.

At this point Paul has come to the end of his first argument that the word of God has not failed because many Jews have not accepted Jesus as the Messiah. God may have chosen to show mercy only to some Jews, along with Gentiles, and hardened the hearts of the remaining Jews. This naturally leads Paul to ask whether God has rejected God's people. Paul's answer is an emphatic no (11:1). Paul supports this in two ways.

First, in 11:1–6 he points again to the existence of Jews who have accepted Jesus as the Messiah, a remnant (v. 5) that includes himself (v. 1). Earlier he mentioned this group as he talked about God's freedom to choose among those who belong to Israel by birth. Now he uses it to show that God has not completely rejected God's people.

Second, in 11:7–34 he discusses the Jews who have not accepted Jesus as the Messiah, those whose hearts God has hardened (v. 7). In verse 11 Paul asks if unbelieving Jews have stumbled so as to fall, and answers no.

> 11 So I ask, have they stumbled so as to fall? By no means! But through their stumbling salvation has come to the Gentiles, so as to make Israel jealous. 12 Now if their stumbling means riches for the world, and if their defeat means riches for Gentiles, how much more will their full inclusion mean! 13 Now I am speaking to you Gentiles. Inasmuch then as I am an apostle to the Gentiles, I glorify my ministry 14 in order to make my own people jealous, and thus save some of them. 15 For if their rejection is the reconciliation of the world, what will their acceptance be but life from the dead! 16 If the part of the dough offered as first fruits is holy, then the whole batch is holy; and if the root is holy, then the branches also are holy....25 So that you may not claim to be wiser than you are, brothers and sisters, I want you to understand this mystery: a hardening has come upon part of Israel, until the full number of the Gentiles has come in. 26 And so all Israel will be saved; as it is written, "Out of Zion will come the Deliverer; he will banish ungodliness from Jacob." 27 "And this is my covenant with them, when I take away their sins." 28 As regards the gospel they are enemies of God for your sake; but as regards election they are beloved, for the sake of their ancestors; 29 for the gifts and the calling of God are irrevocable. 30 Just as you were once disobedient to God but have now received mercy because of their disobedience, 31 so they have now been disobedient in order that, by the mercy shown to you, they too may now receive mercy.

Their unbelief has not caused them to be lost but is part of God's plan. Mysteriously, God has hardened part of Israel in order to bring about the salvation of Gentiles. Just as God hardened the heart of Pharaoh for a good purpose (9:17–18), so God hardened part of Israel for a good purpose. Paul presupposes that if all Israel had accepted Jesus as the Messiah, salvation would not have come to the Gentiles; the unbelief of part of Israel was necessary so that the Gentiles would be saved. But when the full number of Gentiles has come in, all of Israel will be saved (vv. 11–12, 15, 25–26). Because the gifts and call of God are irrevocable (v. 29), unbelieving Jews will ultimately receive mercy (v. 31). Paul ends by praising the inscrutable wisdom and knowledge of God (vv. 33–36).

Paul speaks about the ultimate salvation of all Israel so that Gentiles will not improperly boast over unbelieving Israel.

> 17 But if some of the branches were broken off, and you, a wild olive shoot, were grafted in their place to share the rich root of the olive tree, 18 do not boast over the branches. If you do boast, remember that it is not you that support the root, but the root that supports you. 19 You will say, "Branches were broken off so that I might be grafted in." 20 That is true. They were broken off because of their unbelief, but you stand only through faith. So do not become proud, but stand in awe. 21 For if God did not spare the natural branches, perhaps he will not spare you. 22 Note then the kindness and the severity of God: severity toward those who have fallen, but God's kindness toward you, provided you continue in his kindness; otherwise you also will be cut off. 23 And even those of Israel, if they do not persist in unbelief, will be grafted in, for God has the power to graft them in again. 24 For if you have been cut from what is by nature a wild olive tree and grafted, contrary to nature, into a cultivated olive tree, how much more will these natural branches be grafted back into their own olive tree.

Gentile Christians need to remember that they are shoots of a wild olive tree that have been grafted into the cultivated olive tree that is Israel (v. 17). They need to remember that they are supported by the root; the root is not supported by them (v. 18). Even though some branches of the cultivated olive tree were broken off to make room for the wild olive shoots, the Gentiles should not boast over these branches (vv. 19–20). Finally, these branches will be grafted back into the tree.

F. HUMANITY IN CHRIST

Our discussion of how Paul understands Christ's death and resurrection as salvific (see "The Action of Christ," above) has brought us to the central idea of Paul's theology—the idea that those who believe in Christ are united with Christ or even identified with him. Paul expresses this idea succinctly in Gal 2:20:

> It is no longer I who live, but it is Christ who lives in me.

This unity between Christ and the believer is both Paul's most important way of understanding how Christ saves humanity and the most important description of the new life believers receive through Christ. We have already seen one indication of the latter in discussing possession of the Holy Spirit as the principal way that Christians presently experience new life with Christ. Christians possess the Holy Spirit because Christ possesses it, and their union with Christ implies that they share Christ's spirit.

This unity between Christ and Christians is sometimes called mystical.[1] Others simply speak of Christians' participation in Christ.[2] The latter is probably preferable because it has fewer potentially misleading connotations.

The unity between Christ and Christians comes to expression in many different ways in the letters of Paul.[3] It underlies references to putting on Christ (Rom 13:14; Gal 3:27), to putting on the new human being (Eph 4:24; Col 3:10), and to Christ's having created in himself one new humanity in place of humanity divided

---

1. E.g., by A. Deissmann, "The Christ-Mystic," in Meeks, ed., *The Writings of St. Paul*, 374–87; Schweitzer, *Mysticism of Paul*; Dibelius, "Mystic and Prophet," in Meeks, *The Writings of St. Paul*, 395–409; A. Wikenhauser, *Pauline Mysticism*, and the encyclical of Pius XII *Mystici Corporis* (1943). The encyclical explains that use of the term "mystical" serves to distinguish the body of the church both from the individual physical body of Christ and from any other physical or moral body.

2. Sanders, *Paul and Palestinian Judaism*, 453–63; Dunn, *Theology of Paul*, 390–412. Cf. Beker, *Paul the Apostle*, 307–13.

3. See Robinson, *The Body*, 58–67.

into Jew and Gentile (Eph 2:15). For example, the last of these passages reads,

> He has abolished the law with its commandments and ordinances, that he might create in himself one new humanity in place of the two, thus making peace.

The unity between Christ and Christians also underlies the reference to being in Christ as a new creation in 2 Cor 5:17 (cf. Gal 6:15).

> So if anyone is in Christ, there is a new creation: everything old has passed away; see, everything has become new!

It also underlies Paul's use of certain prepositional phrases. Most important, Paul frequently speaks of believers as being "in Christ" or "in the Lord," as we can see, for example, in 2 Cor 5:17.[4] As in Gal 2:20, Paul can also speak of Christ being in believers.[5] Paul also frequently refers to believers as being "with Christ." More important than the prepositional phrase are the many words compounded with the preposition "with"; these are characteristic of Paul's writing.[6] For example, in Phil 3:21 Paul says about Jesus,

> He will transform the body of our humiliation that it may be conformed to the body of his glory.

"Conformed to" means "given form along with." Less common expressions of the unity between Christ and believers are the phrases "into Christ" and "through Christ."[7]

---

4. See E. Best, *One Body in Christ*, 1–33; Fitzmyer, *Paul and His Theology*, 89–90; Dunn, *Theology of Paul*, 396–401. Fitzmyer counts 165 instances of these phrases in the letters of Paul, including the phrase "in him" where the antecedent of "him" is Christ. Dunn counts 83 instances of "in Christ" and 47 of "in the Lord."

5. See Rom 8:10; 2 Cor 13:5; Eph 3:17; Col 1:27.

6. See Best, *One Body in Christ*, 44–64; Fitzmyer, *Paul and His Theology*, 89; Dunn, *Theology of Paul*, 401–4. Dunn lists forty "with" compounds.

7. See Best (*One Body in Christ*, 65–73) on "into Christ." Fitzmyer (*Paul and His Theology*, 88–89) and Dunn (*Theology of Paul*, 404–6) discuss both phrases.

Union with Christ in His Death and Resurrection

Although it is not always explicit, the union of Christ and believer is especially union with Christ in his death and resurrection. Thus, immediately before Gal 2:20, quoted above, Paul says,

> I have been crucified with Christ. (Gal 2:19)

In discussing this and other passages above (see "The Action of Christ"), we have seen that it is specifically union with Christ in his death and resurrection that brings freedom from sin. Here we see that the union with Christ that constitutes the new life of Christians is also union with him in death and resurrection.[8] Until salvation is fully accomplished, dying and rising with Christ are an ongoing reality in the life of the Christian.

According to most of the passages that describe union with Christ in death and resurrection as the means of salvation, believers have already died with Christ and entered upon a new life, but resurrection with Christ still lies in the future (cf. 2 Tim 2:11). Another passage in which Paul speaks of the believer's resurrection with Christ as a future event is 2 Cor 4:14. From this perspective, the life of Christians lies between their death with Christ and resurrection with him.

In Eph 2:5–6 and Col 2:12; 3:1, not only death with Christ but also resurrection with him are presented as past events. The last of these passages reads,

> So if you have been raised with Christ, seek the things that are above, where Christ is, seated at the right hand of God.

In these passages, however, the incompleteness of union with Christ in death and resurrection is expressed by saying that the full

---

8. R. C. Tannehill entitles two of the sections of his book *Dying and Rising with Christ* "Dying with Christ as the Basis of the New Life" and "Dying and Rising with Christ as the Structure of the New Life."

effects of dying and rising with Christ have not yet been revealed. Ephesians 2:7 says that Christians were raised with Christ

> so that in the ages to come [God] might show the immeasurable riches of his grace in kindness toward [them] in Christ Jesus.

Colossians 3:3–4 says that although they have been raised with Christ, the life of Christians is now hidden and will be revealed when Christ is revealed at his second coming. From this perspective, the life of Christians lies between their death and resurrection with Christ, on the one hand, and the full manifestation of this at the second coming of Christ, on the other.

Paul also speaks of dying and rising with Christ as a process that extends throughout the life of the Christian. In 2 Cor 4:10–11 Paul says of himself and other apostles,

> [We are] always carrying in the body the death of Jesus, so that the life of Jesus may also be made visible in our bodies. For while we live, we are always being given up to death for Jesus' sake, so that the life of Jesus may be made visible in our mortal flesh.

This understanding of Christian life as ongoing participation in the death and resurrection of Christ also underlies other passages in 2 Corinthians.[9] Likewise, in Rom 8:17 Paul says that Christians are joint heirs with Christ

> if, in fact, we suffer with him so that we may also be glorified with him.

And in Phil 3:10–11 he says,

> I want to know Christ and the power of his resurrection and the sharing of his sufferings by becoming like him in his death, if somehow I may attain the resurrection from the dead.

---

9. 2 Cor 1:3–9; 7:3; 12:9; 13:4 (Tannehill, *Dying and Rising with Christ*, 90–100). Tannehill argues that the imitation of the Lord in 1 Thess 1:5–8; 2:13–16 is also a matter of ongoing death and resurrection with Christ (pp. 100–104). On suffering as a participation in the death of Christ, see also Schweitzer, *Mysticism of Paul*, 141–59.

Second Corinthians 4:8–9 suggests that ongoing participation in the death and resurrection of Christ is a matter of undergoing various sufferings without being overwhelmed by them.

> We are afflicted in every way, but not crushed; perplexed, but not driven to despair; persecuted, but not forsaken; struck down, but not destroyed.

Second Corinthians 12:9–10 also suggests that participating in the death of Christ is a matter of experiencing various difficulties. Second Corinthians 1:3–9 and 7:3–4 imply that dying and rising with Christ occurs in the experience of affliction and consolation. First Thessalonians 1:5–8 and 2:13–16 may imply that experiencing persecution is dying with Christ. From this perspective, the life of Christians is a continuous process of dying and rising with Christ.

Thus Christians have died but not yet risen with Christ; or their death and resurrection with Christ has not yet been revealed; or their life is an ongoing death and resurrection with Christ. All of this is so because salvation has not yet fully arrived. At the second coming of Jesus, Christians will simply enjoy resurrection life with him. Until that time Christians already enjoy salvation but do not yet fully enjoy it. Paul says either that they exist between their death with Christ and resurrection with him, or that they await full manifestation of their resurrection with Christ, or that they continuously die and rise with Christ.

The Body of Christ

Paul's most important way of expressing the unity of believers with Christ, especially in his death and resurrection, is to say that they are incorporated into Christ, that they become part of the body of Christ.[10] He discusses the body of Christ in several different connections.

---

10. See Robinson, *The Body*, 49–55; Best, *One Body in Christ*, 83–159.

1. Baptism

Paul nowhere describes exactly what was said and done in baptism.[11] It is possible, however, to infer some features of the ritual from his various references to it. Wayne Meeks sums up these inferences as follows.[12] The word "baptism" itself indicates that the center of the ritual was a water bath, probably either by immersion in a river (cf. Acts 16:13–15) or by pouring water over the person being baptized as he or she stood in a tub. The person being baptized probably disrobed, was baptized naked, and put his or her clothes back on afterward. Baptism may have been accompanied by anointing that symbolized the gift of the Holy Spirit (cf. 2 Cor 1:21); in any case, it was certainly associated somehow with the gift of the Holy Spirit. Baptism may have been accompanied by a formal confession of faith.

Even if our knowledge of the baptismal ritual is rather limited, Paul clearly expresses the meaning of baptism. Baptism incorporates the person baptized into the body of Christ in the one Spirit (1 Cor 12:12–13).

> 12 For just as the body is one and has many members, and all the members of the body, though many, are one body, so it is with Christ. 13 For in the one Spirit we were all baptized into one body—Jews or Greeks, slaves or free and we were all made to drink of one Spirit.

In baptism one puts on Christ (Gal 3:27). Therefore in baptism one also dies with Christ, is buried with him, and enters into new life with him (Rom 6:3–11; Col 2:12).

> 3 Do you not know that all of us who have been baptized into Christ Jesus were baptized into his death? 4 Therefore we have been buried with him by baptism into death, so that, just as

---

11. On baptism in Paul, see Bultmann, *Theology of the New Testament*, 1:311–13; cf. 140–44; Schoeps, *Paul*, 110–15; Bornkamm, *Paul*, 188–90; Ridderbos, *Paul*, 396–414; Conzelmann, *Outline*, 271–73; Meeks, *First Urban Christians*, 150–57; Fitzmyer, *Paul and His Theology*, 86–88; Dunn, *Theology of Paul*, 442–59.

12. Meeks, *First Urban Christians*, 150–52.

> Christ was raised from the dead by the glory of the Father, so
> we too might walk in newness of life. (Rom 6:3–4)

Because baptism unites the believer with Christ, what has happened
to Christ has also happened to the believer. This is particularly true
of the central events of Christ's life, namely, his death and resurrection.

Baptism creates an intimate union between Christ and the
believer but also an intimate union among believers. Because persons who believe and are baptized are identified with Christ, all
such persons are also identified with one another by virtue of their
common identification with Christ. The logic of this can be represented thus: if believer a = Christ and believer b = Christ, then
believer a = believer b.

Because baptism creates an intimate relationship with Christ
and therefore with all others who believe in him, baptism entails
negation of formerly meaningful distinctions among people.[13] In
Gal 3:27–28 Paul says,

> 27 As many of you as were baptized into Christ have clothed
> yourselves with Christ. 28 There is no longer Jew or Greek,
> there is no longer slave or free, there is no longer male and
> female; for all of you are one in Christ Jesus.

Compare also 1 Cor 12:13. Colossians 3:11 is similar but lacks
explicit reference to baptism. Baptism, however, probably underlies
the reference to putting off the old human being and putting on the
new in 3:9–10. Ephesians 2:11–22 argues at length that the distinction between Jew and Gentile has been negated in Christ.

This negation of formerly meaningful distinctions does not
mean that all Christians become identical. Rather, once the old distinctions have been negated, they are replaced by new distinctions
created as the Spirit gives different gifts to each (1 Cor 12:4–11).

> 7 To each is given the manifestation of the Spirit for the com-
> mon good.... 11 All these are activated by one and the same

---

13. On negation of distinctions within the church, see Beker, *Paul the Apostle*,
322–27.

Spirit, who allots to each one individually just as the Spirit chooses. (1 Cor 12:7, 11)

These different gifts work together like the parts of the human body, as we will discuss below (see "Church").

The negation of old distinctions and the creation of new ones is one aspect of dying and rising with Christ. As Christians die with Christ, they leave behind the things that formerly distinguished them from one another, along with slavery to sin and death. As they enter into new life with Christ, they are given mutually interdependent gifts of the Spirit so that they form the body of Christ.

It comes as no surprise that putting into practice the negation of old distinctions and the creation of new ones was problematic in Paul's communities. We will discuss problems connected with the new distinctions below (in "Church"). Paul at many places in his letters confronts problems connected with negation of the old distinctions.

One aspect of negation of the distinction between Jew and Gentile underlies Paul's argument in Galatians, Romans, and Philippians that Gentile Christians should not keep the Jewish law. Paul makes the argument because Gentiles are drawn to keeping the Jewish law even though the distinction has been eliminated. In Gal 2:11–14 Paul recounts an occasion when he confronted Cephas for failing to continue eating with Gentiles as a way of living out the implications of the negation.

> 11 But when Cephas came to Antioch, I opposed him to his face, because he stood self-condemned; 12 for until certain people came from James, he used to eat with the Gentiles. But after they came, he drew back and kept himself separate for fear of the circumcision faction. 13 And the other Jews joined him in this hypocrisy, so that even Barnabas was led astray by their hypocrisy. 14 But when I saw that they were not acting consistently with the truth of the gospel, I said to Cephas before them all, "If you, though a Jew, live like a Gentile and not like a Jew, how can you compel the Gentiles to live like Jews?"

In 1 Cor 7:18–19 Paul argues that the circumcised person should not remove the marks of circumcision nor should the uncircumcised be circumcised.

> 18 Was anyone at the time of his call already circumcised? Let him not seek to remove the marks of circumcision. Was anyone at the time of his call uncircumcised? Let him not seek circumcision. 19 Circumcision is nothing, and uncircumcision is nothing; but obeying the commandments of God is everything.

Throughout Romans, and especially in 11:13–32, Paul seems to try to counter Gentile boasting over unbelieving Israel; he regards this as taking the negation too far. We see something similar in Eph 2:11–22.

Paul deals with an aspect of the negation of the distinction between slave and free in 1 Cor 7:21–24, where he seems to urge slaves not to seek freedom from their masters.

> 21 Were you a slave when called? Do not be concerned about it. Even if you can gain your freedom, make use of your present condition now more than ever. 22 For whoever was called in the Lord as a slave is a freed person belonging to the Lord, just as whoever was free when called is a slave of Christ. 23 You were bought with a price; do not become slaves of human masters. 24 In whatever condition you were called, brothers and sisters, there remain with God.

The Letter to Philemon addresses another aspect of this negation. Paul asks Philemon not to punish his runaway slave Onesimus (vv. 17–19) and strongly suggests that Philemon should send Onesimus back to Paul (vv. 13–14). Paul deals with other aspects of negation of the distinction between slave and free in Eph 6:5–9 and Col 3:22–4:1. (See "Ethics," below).

Finally, Paul deals with an aspect of the negation of the distinction between male and female in 1 Cor 7:2–16, where he carefully parallels everything he says to husbands with the same thing said to wives. For example, in verses 3–4 he says,

> 3 The husband should give to his wife her conjugal rights, and likewise the wife to her husband. 4 For the wife does not have

authority over her own body, but the husband does; likewise the husband does not have authority over his own body, but the wife does.

In 11:2–16 and 14:34–35 Paul seems to counter behavior that he sees as taking the negation too far. In the former passage, he argues that women should dress differently than men when praying or prophesying; in the latter, he argues that wives should be silent at some gatherings of believers. Paul deals with other aspects of negation of the distinction between men and women in Eph 5:22–33 and Col 3:18–19. (See "Ethics," below.)

2. Eucharist

Paul provides even less information about what was said and done in celebrating the Eucharist than he does about baptism.[14] Meeks summarizes as follows what can be inferred.[15] The basic action was the eating of a common meal, at which it was possible that "one goes hungry and another becomes drunk" (1 Cor 11:21). Paul quotes a sacred formula used in the celebration in 1 Cor 11:23–26. From this formula we can infer that this meal imitated the meal of Jesus with his disciples on the night he was betrayed. After a thanksgiving, bread was broken and distributed with the formula "This is my body that is for you. Do this in remembrance of me." Then, perhaps at the end of the meal, a cup was passed with the formula "This cup is the new covenant in my blood. Do this, as often as you drink it, in remembrance of me."

Although few details of the ritual are certain, Paul expresses the meaning of the Eucharist rather clearly. Like baptism, participation in the Eucharist incorporates the participant into the body of Christ. In 1 Cor 10:16 Paul asks,

---

14. On Eucharist in Paul, see Bultmann, *Theology of the New Testament*, 1:313–14; cf. 146–49; Schoeps, *Paul*, 115–18; Bornkamm, *Paul*, 190–93; Ridderbos, *Paul*, 414–28; Conzelmann, *Outline*, 273–74; Meeks, *First Urban Christians*, 157–62; Fitzmyer, *Paul and His Theology*, 93–95; Dunn, *Theology of Paul*, 600–623. Cf. *Mystici Corporis* 81–84.

15. Meeks, *First Urban Christians*, 157–59.

> The cup of blessing that we bless, is it not a sharing in the blood of Christ? The bread that we break, is it not a sharing in the body of Christ?

Drinking the eucharistic cup is a participation in the blood of Christ; eating the eucharistic bread is a participation in the body of Christ. Paul does not explicitly say why. In 1 Cor 11:23–25, however, Paul recalls that on the night he was betrayed, Jesus gave people bread and wine, saying that it was his body and blood, and told them to do this in memory of him.

> 23 For I received from the Lord what I also handed on to you, that the Lord Jesus on the night when he was betrayed took a loaf of bread, 24 and when he had given thanks, he broke it and said, "This is my body that is for you. Do this in remembrance of me." 25 In the same way he took the cup also, after supper, saying, "This cup is the new covenant in my blood. Do this, as often as you drink it, in remembrance of me."

This strongly suggests that when Christians do this in memory of Jesus, the eucharistic bread and wine are the body and blood of Jesus; therefore consuming the eucharistic bread and wine unites the one consuming with the body and blood of Christ.

Also like baptism, participation in the Eucharist is union with Christ in death and resurrection. When Christians celebrate the Eucharist, they recall the events of the night Jesus was betrayed, which were soon followed by Jesus' death and resurrection. The words of Jesus they recall speak of the bread as Jesus' body that is for them, and the cup as the new covenant in his blood (11:24–25). This suggests that when Jesus first gave people bread and wine as his body and blood, he was looking forward to his death and interpreting it as an act for their benefit. His death would create a new covenant between God and humanity. This is why Paul says in 11:26,

> For as often as you eat this bread and drink the cup, you proclaim the Lord's death until he comes.

Celebrating the Eucharist is remembrance of Jesus' Last Supper and his subsequent death and resurrection, and a participation in that death and resurrection. Therefore the celebration is a proclamation of Jesus' death until he comes again. The resurrection is presupposed.

And finally, like baptism, participation in the Eucharist is simultaneously an intimate union between the individual believer and Christ and an intimate union among believers. Thus in 1 Cor 10:17 Paul says,

> Because there is one bread, we who are many are one body, for we all partake of the one bread.

It is especially striking that Paul mentions this here because it does not contribute to his argument at this point. At this point he is only concerned to argue that Eucharist is a matter of union with Christ. Union with Christ and union among believers are so closely connected in Paul's mind, however, that he mentions the latter alongside the former even when it does not serve his immediate purpose.

The way the Eucharist unites all of those who partake of it into the body of Christ is basic to Paul's discussion of the Corinthian celebration of it in 1 Cor 11:17–34.

> 17 Now in the following instructions I do not commend you, because when you come together it is not for the better but for the worse. 18 For, to begin with, when you come together as a church, I hear that there are divisions among you; and to some extent I believe it.... 20 When you come together, it is not really to eat the Lord's supper. 21 For when the time comes to eat, each of you goes ahead with your own supper, and one goes hungry and another becomes drunk. 22 What! Do you not have homes to eat and drink in? Or do you show contempt for the church of God and humiliate those who have nothing? What should I say to you? Should I commend you? In this matter I do not commend you!... 27 Whoever, therefore, eats the bread or drinks the cup of the Lord in an unworthy manner will be answerable for the body and blood of the Lord. 28 Examine yourselves, and only then eat of the bread and drink of the cup. 29 For all who eat and drink without discerning the body, eat and drink judgment against themselves. 30 For this reason many of you are weak and ill, and some have died. 31 But if we judged ourselves, we would not be judged.

32 But when we are judged by the Lord, we are disciplined so that we may not be condemned along with the world. 33 So then, my brothers and sisters, when you come together to eat, wait for one another. 34 If you are hungry, eat at home, so that when you come together, it will not be for your condemnation. About the other things I will give instructions when I come.

What Paul finds problematic is divisions among the Corinthians when they celebrate the Eucharist (v. 18). These divisions consist of unequal participation in the meal such that each goes ahead with his or her own supper and one goes hungry while another becomes drunk (v. 21). Paul considers this eating the bread and drinking the cup of the Lord in an unworthy manner (v. 27). It consists of eating and drinking without discerning the body (v. 29). That is, the Corinthians fail to discern themselves as the body of Christ, united as such by the Eucharist itself. This way of celebrating the Eucharist contradicts its essential character. Paul warns that those who celebrate in this way "will be answerable for the body and blood of the Lord" (v. 27). They "eat and drink judgment on themselves" (v. 29). And Paul suggests that the Corinthians are already experiencing sickness and death because of this (v. 30).

No doubt Paul would see other ways of failing to discern the body of Christ properly as one celebrates the Eucharist. In 1 Corinthians, however, the failure that concerns him is failure to manifest the union among believers that exists because of their common union with Christ.

For Paul, baptism and Eucharist both have the same fundamental meaning. Both are incorporation into the body of Christ, especially into his death and resurrection. Both are simultaneously union with Christ and with others who are united to Christ. One difference between them is that baptism occurs only once whereas the Eucharist is celebrated repeatedly. Perhaps Paul sees baptism as the beginning of incorporation into Christ, and the Eucharist as a repeated renewal of that incorporation.

3. Church

Paul discusses the union of believers in the body of Christ at greatest length in specifying the nature of the relationship among them.[16] Like the members of the human body, they are mutually interdependent. In discussing this, Paul does not explicitly refer to their union with Christ in death and resurrection. As we have seen above in "Baptism," however, Paul understands the relationship among the members of the body of Christ as a result of death and resurrection with Christ. Their existence as members of the body of Christ is an aspect of entering into new life in union with Christ after having died with him.

Paul's most extensive treatment of the relationship among the members of the body of Christ is found in 1 Cor 12:12–31. This passage is part of a long discussion of spiritual gifts in chapters 12–14. These are the new distinctions among Christians, created by the Spirit, that replace the distinctions negated by baptism (see "Baptism," above). Paul's main point in this discussion is that the Spirit gives different gifts to different Christians; all do not have the same gifts (12:4–11). It becomes clear in chapter 14, where Paul argues that speaking in tongues is inferior to prophecy, that the Corinthians especially emphasize the gift of speaking in tongues. Perhaps the Corinthians thought that everyone needed to have the gift of speaking in tongues and that it was an essential sign of their possession of the Holy Spirit (12:3). Against such a view, Paul argues that the Holy Spirit gives a variety of gifts, not the same gift to everyone.

In 12:12–31 Paul makes this point by means of a detailed comparison of the church to a human body.

> 12 For just as the body is one and has many members, and all the members of the body, though many, are one body, so it is with Christ. 13 For in the one Spirit we were all baptized into one body—Jews or Greeks, slaves or free—and we were all made to drink of one Spirit. 14 Indeed, the body does not consist of one member but of many.... 27 Now you are the body of Christ and individually members of it. 28 And God has appointed in the church first apostles, second prophets, third teachers; then deeds of power, then gifts of healing, forms of

---

16. On the church in Paul, see Bultmann, *Theology of the New Testament*, 1:310–11; Ridderbos, *Paul*, 362–95, 438–80; Conzelmann, *Outline*, 259–65; Fitzmyer, *Paul and His Theology*, 95–97; Dunn, *Theology of Paul*, 534–64.

assistance, forms of leadership, various kinds of tongues. 29 Are all apostles? Are all prophets? Are all teachers? Do all work miracles? 30 Do all possess gifts of healing? Do all speak in tongues? Do all interpret?

Just as the human body has many members all combining to form one body, so it is with Christ (v. 12). God gives Christians different gifts (vv. 28–30), thus making each person different as the members of the human body differ. All of these different gifts must be combined and work together to constitute the body of Christ. Christians "are the body of Christ and individually members of it" (v. 27).

In verses 15–20 Paul says that if one part of the human body, such as the foot, would say it did not belong to the body because it was not some other part of the body, such as a hand, it would not thereby cease to be part of the body. There are many different members, but one body.

> 15 If the foot would say, "Because I am not a hand, I do not belong to the body," that would not make it any less a part of the body. 16 And if the ear would say, "Because I am not an eye, I do not belong to the body," that would not make it any less a part of the body. 17 If the whole body were an eye, where would the hearing be? If the whole body were hearing, where would the sense of smell be? 18 But as it is, God arranged the members in the body, each one of them, as he chose. 19 If all were a single member, where would the body be? 20 As it is, there are many members, yet one body.

This suggests that some in Corinth (the "have-nots") doubted that they possessed the Spirit because they did not speak in tongues. Paul uses the comparison to a body to show the absurdity of that view.

In verses 21–26 Paul says that one part of the human body, such as the eye, cannot say it has no need of some other part of the body, such as the hand.

> 21 The eye cannot say to the hand, "I have no need of you," nor again the head to the feet, "I have no need of you." 22 On the contrary, the members of the body that seem to be weaker

are indispensable, 23 and those members of the body that we think less honorable we clothe with greater honor, and our less respectable members are treated with greater respect; 24 whereas our more respectable members do not need this. But God has so arranged the body, giving the greater honor to the inferior member, 25 that there may be no dissension within the body, but the members may have the same care for one another. 26 If one member suffers, all suffer together with it; if one member is honored, all rejoice together with it.

This suggests that others in Corinth (the "haves") doubted that they needed the members of the church who did not speak in tongues. Again Paul uses the comparison to a body to show the absurdity of that view.

Paul makes a similar argument more briefly and more generally in Rom 12:3–8. In this passage he argues that no Christian should think of himself or herself too highly. God gives Christians different gifts, all of which are needed to constitute the body of Christ. Christians are "one body in Christ, and individually... members of one another" (v. 5).

Paul rather frequently refers to the church as the body of Christ in Colossians and Ephesians.[17] Of these references only Eph 4:11–12 and 15–16 speak of the mutual interdependence of the members of the body. Ephesians 4:11–12 reads,

> 11 The gifts he gave were that some would be apostles, some prophets, some evangelists, some pastors and teachers, 12 to equip the saints for the work of ministry, for building up the body of Christ.

Ephesians 2:15–16 identifies as the body the new humanity created by Christ to replace humanity divided into Jew and Gentile. What is most striking about these passages is that many of them speak of Christ as head of his body, the church. Thus Col 1:18 says of Christ,

> He is the head of the body, the church.[18]

---

17. See Col 1:18, 24; 2:19; 3:15; Eph 1:22–23; 2:15–16; 4:4, 11–12, 15–16.
18. So also Col 2:19; Eph 1:22–23; 4:15–16.

Apart from Colossians and Ephesians, Paul speaks of the church simply as the body of Christ; Christ is identified with the whole body. Only in Colossians and Ephesians is Christ identified with one part of the body, that is, the head. This is often seen as an indication that Paul is not the author of these letters. Assuming that he is the author, he has developed his understanding of the church as the body of Christ in a new way in these letters.

In the passages we have been discussing, Paul gives four different lists of the gifts given to Christians by the Spirit.[19] The only gift that appears on all four lists is that of prophecy. Teaching appears on three of the four (i.e., all but 1 Cor 12:8–10). Healing, miracles, tongues and interpretation of tongues appear on both lists in 1 Corinthians; apostle appears on the second of these lists and the list in Ephesians. A total of thirteen other gifts appear on one of the lists. Obviously there is no standard list of spiritual gifts.[20]

One kind of gift that is not well represented is that involved in leading the church. The apostles provided a kind of intermittent leadership, as Paul's own career illustrates.[21] Paul founded churches and provided subsequent guidance through return visits from himself and his associates, and through letters. However, as an itinerant Paul could not provide daily leadership. Unlike the apostles, prophets and teachers may have been continuously present within the churches. The exercise of these gifts would seem to have constituted a type of leadership by their very nature. However, Paul's extensive discussion of prophecy in 1 Corinthians 14 does not suggest that prophets functioned as administrators.

Two of the gifts that Paul mentions once may refer to an administrative function. In 1 Cor 12:28 Paul mentions the gift of administrations (κυβερνήσεις). Since he simply mentions it here and does not refer to it elsewhere, it is difficult to say what this means. In Rom 12:8 Paul mentions the leader (προϊστάμενος). This could refer either to giving aid or to leading. These were two

---

19. See 1 Cor 12:8–10, 28–30; Rom 12:6–8; Eph 4:11.

20. Dunn argues that they can be grouped as gifts of speech and action (*Theology of Paul*, 555).

21. On the leadership of the apostles and others in the Pauline churches, see Meeks, *First Urban Christians*, 111–39; Dunn, *Theology of Paul*, 566–86.

aspects of leadership in the ancient world; leaders were expected to be benefactors. The latter aspect might be suggested by the placement of the word in the Romans list between giving and being compassionate. Paul also uses this term in 1 Thess 5:12, where it may refer to leaders of the Thessalonian community.[22] In Rom 16:2 Paul speaks of Phoebe as a deacon and a benefactor (προστάτις). He also mentions deacons and bishops in Phil 1:1.

In his letters Paul does not seem to presume the existence of leadership in the churches he addresses, to which he can appeal to deal with the various issues he discusses. And as we have just seen, he does not say much about leadership as a gift of the Spirit. Perhaps the heads of the households in which the Christians gathered supplied the minimum of necessary leadership. The household of Stephanas may have played this role in Corinth; in 1 Cor 16:15–16 Paul urges the Corinthians to submit to the members of that household. In 1 Timothy and Titus we can see a movement from leadership of individual households to leadership of the church understood as the household of God.[23]

4. Sex and Marriage

A final context in which Paul discusses his understanding of the church as the body of Christ is in reflecting on sex and marriage.[24] In discussing baptism, Eucharist, and proper relationships among the members of the church, Paul speaks directly about various aspects of the church as the body of Christ. By contrast Paul sees sex and marriage as analogous to the body of Christ. Sex and marriage are not a matter of involvement in the body of Christ. But Paul understands them as creating a union between man and woman that is similar to the union between believers and Christ and among believers. The similarity illuminates both.

---

22. In 1 Timothy the participle is used to describe the leadership of bishops (3:4–5), deacons (3:12), and elders (5:17) both within their own households and in the church, the household of God. On the other hand, the participle is used in Titus 3:8, 14 to speak of devotion to good works.

23. See the citations in the preceding note.

24. See Best, *One Body in Christ*, 169–83; Fitzmyer, *Paul and His Theology*, 91. Cf. *Mystici Corporis* 67.

Paul speaks of the similarity between the union created by sexual intercourse and the body of Christ in 1 Cor 6:12–20.

> 12 "All things are lawful for me," but not all things are beneficial. "All things are lawful for me," but I will not be dominated by anything. 13 "Food is meant for the stomach and the stomach for food," and God will destroy both one and the other. The body is meant not for fornication but for the Lord, and the Lord for the body. 14 And God raised the Lord and will also raise us by his power. 15 Do you not know that your bodies are members of Christ? Should I therefore take the members of Christ and make them members of a prostitute? Never! 16 Do you not know that whoever is united to a prostitute becomes one body with her? For it is said, "The two shall be one flesh." 17 But anyone united to the Lord becomes one spirit with him. 18 Shun fornication! Every sin that a person commits is outside the body; but the fornicator sins against the body itself. 19 Or do you not know that your body is a temple of the Holy Spirit within you, which you have from God, and that you are not your own? 20 For you were bought with a price; therefore glorify God in your body.

In this passage Paul argues that the Corinthians ought not to have sexual intercourse with prostitutes. The Corinthians have apparently justified this behavior by saying, "All things are permitted for me" (v. 12) and "Food is for the belly and the belly for food" (v. 13). The latter seems to imply that the desire for sexual gratification is like the desire for food; both desires can simply be satisfied.

Paul counters this second justification by saying that sexual intercourse is more than simple gratification of desire. The one who has sexual intercourse with a prostitute becomes one body with her (v. 16). Paul bases this on Gen 2:24, "Therefore a man leaves his father and his mother and clings to his wife, and they become one flesh," of which he quotes the final clause. Paul understands this verse as revealing the true nature of sexual intercourse. Whatever two people may think they are doing when they have sexual intercourse, even if they think they are simply gratifying an appetite, in fact their sexual union makes them one body.[25]

---

25. This same understanding of sexual union may be presupposed by the sayings

This is the same union that Christians already have with Christ by virtue of their faith in him. Paul asks the Corinthians if they are unaware that their bodies are members of Christ and if it is appropriate to make the members of Christ members of a prostitute (v. 15). The parallel between the union of believers with Christ and the union created by sexual intercourse with a prostitute makes it clear that the latter is inappropriate. Once one realizes the significance of sexual intercourse with a prostitute, one also realizes that one should not do it.

In verse 18 Paul urges the Corinthians to flee sexual immorality because, unlike any other sin, it is a sin against one's own body. Because sexual intercourse makes two people into one body, improper sexual intercourse is a violation of one's very self. This is the self that is part of the body of Christ and is destined to be raised by God (v. 14).

First Corinthians 6:12–20 presents an understanding of the nature of sexual intercourse that is potentially very positive, but uses it only to reject improper sexual intercourse. Ephesians 5:25–33 develops the positive potential of this understanding of sexual intercourse.

> 25 Husbands, love your wives, just as Christ loved the church and gave himself up for her, 26 in order to make her holy by cleansing her with the washing of water by the word, 27 so as to present the church to himself in splendor, without a spot or wrinkle or anything of the kind—yes, so that she may be holy and without blemish. 28 In the same way, husbands should love their wives as they do their own bodies. He who loves his wife loves himself. 29 For no one ever hates his own body, but he nourishes and tenderly cares for it, just as Christ does for the church, 30 because we are members of his body. 31 "For this reason a man will leave his father and mother and be joined to his wife, and the two will become one flesh." 32 This is a great mystery, and I am applying it to Christ and the

---

of Jesus found in Mark 10:6–9/Matt 19:4–6, in which Gen 2:24 is cited at the basis for Jesus' prohibition of divorce. Paul may have known these sayings. It is clear from 1 Cor 7:10–11 that Paul did know about Jesus' prohibition of divorce.

church. 33 Each of you, however, should love his wife as himself, and a wife should respect her husband.

In this passage Paul argues that husbands should love their wives as Christ loved the church (v. 25). In verse 28 he says that this means loving their wives as they do their own bodies, as they love themselves. This is the way Christ loved the church, since Christians are members of his body (vv. 29–30). In support of this, Paul quotes Gen 2:24 and applies it to the union of Christ with the church (vv. 31–32).

The union of Christ and church in one body is like the union of husband and wife in one body. When Christ loves the church, he loves himself; likewise, when husbands love their wives, they love themselves. Because of this, husbands can pattern their behavior on that of Christ toward the church. But also because of this, the relationship of husbands and wives makes visible the nature of the relationship between Christ and the church. Paul uses Gen 2:24, which says that man and woman become one flesh, to explicate the union of Christ with the church. Man and woman become one flesh through sexual intercourse. Thus it is the sexual union of husband and wife that manifests the union of Christ with the church.

Not only is the relationship of husband and wife like that of Christ and the church in being a union in one body; they are also alike in that they involve death and implicitly resurrection. Christ gave himself up, that is, was crucified, for his body the church. Christ's resurrection is not mentioned but is presupposed because it is union with Christ in death and resurrection that makes the church his body. In the same way, husbands should love their wives as they do their own bodies. Their love should be like that of Christ in undergoing death for the sake of their wives. Insofar as their death is like that of Christ, it will be followed by resurrection.

In 2 Cor 11:2 Paul says that he betrothed the Corinthians to Christ, again using marriage as an image of the relationship of Christ and the church.

I feel a divine jealousy for you, for I promised you in marriage to one husband, to present you as a chaste virgin to Christ.

144

Though he probably presupposes it, Paul does not explicitly mention that the church is the body of Christ in this passage. Marriage is often used as an image for the union between God and people in the Hebrew scriptures, though not in the specific way Paul uses it.[26] For example, Isa 62:5 reads,

> For as a young man marries a young woman, so shall your builder marry you, and as the bridegroom rejoices over the bride, so shall your God rejoice over you.

---

26. See Hos 2:19–20; Jer 3:1, Ezek 16:6–43; Isa 54:5–6; 62:5.

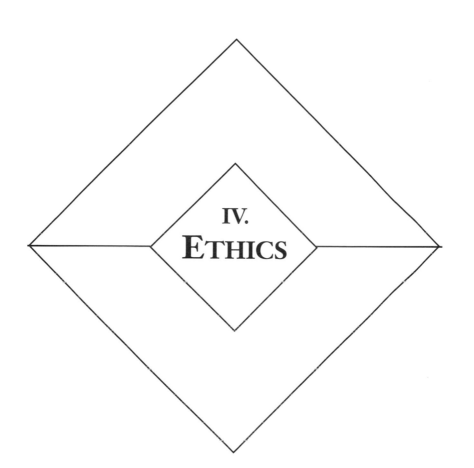

IV.
ETHICS

Foundation

As we have seen, Paul understands salvation as a free gift of God. By incorporating people into Christ, God brings them to the proper goal of human life. This does not depend on anything people have done to deserve it; rather God saves them although they are incapable of deserving it.

This renders Paul's ethical teaching problematic, as his own communities realized. If salvation does not depend on what one does, it seems that one's behavior is indifferent; one can do as one pleases. Paul does not agree. Even though salvation is a free gift, one's behavior does matter. In Rom 6:15 Paul asks a question he assumes is on the mind of those he addresses, "Should we sin because we are not under law but under grace?" His answer is an emphatic no.

Paul bases his ethical teaching on the view that having received salvation from God as a free gift implies a certain way of living. This can be expressed by saying that the imperative follows from the indicative. What one should do (the imperative) is based on one's having been saved by God (the indicative).[1] The opposite relationship between indicative and imperative is more intuitively obvious. It makes more sense that one would behave in a certain way (the imperative) in order to bring about a certain state of affairs (the indicative). This is precluded by Paul's understanding of the situation of human beings apart from Christ, which means that they could not behave in such a way that they achieved salvation. Having received salvation as a gift (the indicative), however, does imply ethical norms (the imperative).

At a very basic level, the reason for this is that salvation is not complete. If salvation had fully arrived for Christians, there would

---

1. For this understanding of the foundation of Paul's ethics, see Bultmann, *Theology of the New Testament*, 1:332–33; cf. 140–44; Furnish, *Theology and Ethics*, 224–27; Bornkamm, *Paul*, 201–5; Ridderbos, *Paul*, 253–58; Beker, *Paul the Apostle*, 255–56, 275–78; Fitzmyer, *Paul and His Theology*, 97–100; Dunn, *Theology of Paul*, 626–31.

be no more need for ethics. But since salvation will only be fully accomplished at the second coming of Jesus, it is necessary to behave in a way appropriate for those who have already died and risen with Christ but await the fullness of union with him. This is true in both a positive and a negative sense.

1. Negative

As we have seen, apart from Christ, human beings are enslaved to sin and death. While they are slaves to sin and death, humans can only serve sin; they are not free to act otherwise. Dying and rising with Christ set them free from sin and death. Now for the first time they can live a good life. But since they are free, they can also reenslave themselves to sin. Their freedom from sin and death in Christ makes ethics meaningful. While they were slaves, no ethical instruction could make it possible for them to behave well. This is why the law was not salvific. Now that they are free in Christ, they can for the first time act in accord with ethical norms.

Freedom from sin and death not only makes ethics meaningful; this freedom makes ethics necessary. If humans are to avoid reenslaving themselves to sin and death, they must behave properly. They must act in such a way that they do not negate their salvation. E. P. Sanders expresses this negative foundation for ethics in Paul by distinguishing between "getting in" and "staying in." Getting in to the community of the redeemed is not based on one's behavior; it is the free gift of God. Staying in that community is based on one's behavior.[2]

Paul expresses this point of view briefly in 1 Cor 6:12 and 10:23.

> "All things are lawful for me," but not all things are beneficial. "All things are lawful for me," but I will not be dominated by anything. (1 Cor 6:12)

In both of these passages Paul apparently quotes a statement the Corinthians use to justify their behavior, "All things are permitted for me." Paul does not contradict this statement; he agrees that

---

2. Sanders, *Paul and Palestinian Judaism*, 513. On the ethical implications of freedom from sin and death, see Conzelmann, *Outline*, 275–82.

Christians are not under a law that prohibits or mandates certain behavior. But in both passages he qualifies the statement by saying that although all things are permitted, "not all things are beneficial." In 1 Cor 6:12 he quotes the statement a second time and qualifies it by saying, "I will not be dominated by anything." There is no law that Christians must keep in order to be followers of Christ. But there are things they can do as followers of Christ that negate the freedom they have received through Christ. Obviously they ought to avoid doing these things.

Paul discusses this negative foundation for ethics at some length in Rom 6:12–23. In Rom 6:1–11 Paul argues that, in union with Christ, Christians have died to sin and entered into new life (see "The Action of Christ," above). This is the indicative, the freedom from sin and death that Christians have received as a gift from God without doing anything but accept it by believing in Jesus. From this indicative flows the imperative in verse 12:

> Therefore, do not let sin exercise dominion in your mortal bodies.

Christians have been set free from sin but can return to slavery. Thus it is necessary for Paul to urge them not to do so. Paul goes on in verses 15–23 to argue that to use one's freedom to sin is to lose that freedom (v. 16). Slavery to sin does not produce good fruit (vv. 19, 21, 23). Paul presumes that if one understands that sin is slavery, one will choose to continue in Christian freedom, not return to slavery.

2. Positive

The imperative also follows upon the indicative in another sense. Not only must Christians avoid negating their salvation; they must also behave in a way that is positively appropriate to their new situation as persons saved by God through Christ. They should respond to the love God has shown them by loving in return. As members of the body of Christ, they should behave like members of Christ. Paul expresses this briefly in 1 Cor 10:23.

> "All things are lawful," but not all things are beneficial. "All things are lawful," but not all things build up.

In this verse Paul's second qualification of the Corinthians' statement, "All things are permitted for me," is "but not all things build up." Some things that Christians might do build up the body of Christ; others do not. Christians should do the things that build up the body of Christ.

Ethics is important for Paul. All of his letters include substantial amounts of ethical exhortation, and 1 Corinthians is almost exclusively devoted to it. Ethics, however, is based on, and secondary to, salvation through Christ. This may be indicated by the placement of the exhortation section of Paul's letters at the end.

Images of Christian Life

Here we will discuss four images for Christian living Paul uses in his letters. Examining these images will help us understand further the relationship between indicative and imperative in both positive and negative senses. The first of the four images embodies the negative foundation for ethics; the others embody the positive foundation.

1. Slavery to Righteousness/God/Christ

The most extensive passage in which Paul develops the image of Christian living as slavery is Rom 6:16–22.[3]

> 16 Do you not know that if you present yourselves to anyone as obedient slaves, you are slaves of the one whom you obey, either of sin, which leads to death, or of obedience, which leads to righteousness? 17 But thanks be to God that you, having once been slaves of sin, have become obedient from the heart to the form of teaching to which you were entrusted, 18 and that you, having been set free from sin, have become slaves of righteousness. 19 I am speaking in human terms because of your natural limitations. For just as you once presented your

---

3. On this see Bultmann, *Theology of the New Testament*, 1:331–32.

members as slaves to impurity and to greater and greater iniq-
uity, so now present your members as slaves to righteousness
for sanctification. 20 When you were slaves of sin, you were
free in regard to righteousness. 21 So what advantage did you
then get from the things of which you now are ashamed? The
end of those things is death. 22 But now that you have been
freed from sin and enslaved to God, the advantage you get is
sanctification. The end is eternal life.

In verse 16 Paul speaks of Christians as slaves of the obedience that
leads to righteousness. In verses 18–19 he simply speaks of the
Christian as a slave to righteousness. Finally in verse 22 Paul speaks
of the Christian as one who has been enslaved to God, which is the
same thing as being a slave to righteousness. Paul also says that
Christians serve God as slaves in 1 Thess 1:9 (cf. Titus 1:1). In Rom
7:6 he states that Christians serve as slaves in newness of spirit.

Elsewhere Paul speaks of being a slave of Christ. In 1 Cor 7:22
Paul says,

> For whoever was called in the Lord as a slave is a freed person
> belonging to the Lord, just as whoever was free when called is
> a slave of Christ.

Paul refers to himself as a slave of Christ in Rom 1:1 and elsewhere,[4] and to others as slaves of Christ in Eph 6:6–7 and elsewhere.[5] The idea that Christians are slaves of Christ probably also
underlies Paul's references to their belonging to Christ. We find
this in many passages,[6] including 1 Cor 3:23, where Paul says to the
Corinthians,

---

4. See Gal 1:10; Phil 1:1.

5. See Phil 1:1 (Timothy); Col 4:7 (Tychicus), 12 (Epaphras); cf. 2 Tim 2:24. In
1 Cor 6:20 and 7:23 Paul says that the Corinthians were bought with a price, perhaps meaning that Christ or God purchased them as slaves. In Phil 2:22 Paul says
that Timothy joined with him in serving the gospel as a slave. Paul speaks of
Christians' serving the Lord as slaves in Rom 12:11, and serving Christ as slaves in
Rom 14:18; 16:18; Col 3:24.

6. See 1 Cor 1:12; 3:23; 15:23; 2 Cor 10:7; Gal 3:29; 5:24. In Rom 14:8 Paul says
that Christians belong to the Lord.

You belong to Christ.

Finally, Paul also refers to Christians as slaves of one another, developing one implication of the idea that they are slaves of Christ. Thus in 1 Cor 9:19 Paul says about himself,

> For though I am free with respect to all, I have made myself a slave to all, so that I might win more of them.

Paul says something similar to this in 2 Cor 4:5. In Gal 5:13 he urges the Galatians to serve one another as slaves.

This image of Christian life expresses the need to avoid negating salvation. Apart from Christ humans are slaves to sin, unable to do anything but sin. Through Christ humans have been set free from sin. Now they can either live uprightly or sin. If they do the latter, they lose the freedom they have gained in Christ. The only way to remain free is to live uprightly. As long as they do so, they retain the freedom to continue doing so or to reenslave themselves to sin. Thus, in order to remain free, they must choose to serve God alone, that is, to be slaves to righteousness, to God, to Christ.[7] Only the service of God is freedom.

2. Walking according to the Spirit

In Rom 8:4 Paul describes Christians as ones who walk according to the Spirit and not according to the flesh.[8]

> [Christians] walk not according to the flesh but according to the Spirit.

---

7. There is some similarity between this view and the saying of Jesus in Matt 6:24/Luke 16:13: "No one can serve two masters; for a slave will either hate the one and love the other, or be devoted to the one and despise the other. You cannot serve God and wealth." This saying presupposes, rather than argues, that one should serve God. But like Paul, it seems to assume that human beings cannot choose whether to serve someone but only whom to serve.

8. On walking according to the Spirit, see Bultmann, *Theology of the New Testament*, 1:336–39; Dunn, *Theology of Paul*, 642–49.

Similarly, in Gal 5:16 Paul urges the Galatians to walk in the Spirit (cf. also Gal 5:25). Paul also speaks of being led by the Spirit in Rom 8:13–14 and Gal 5:18.

This image of Christian life is the best expression of the way the imperative follows upon the indicative in a positive sense. As we have seen, the principal way that Christians presently experience new life with Christ is possession of the Spirit. By dying and rising with Christ, they have received the Spirit of Christ, which is also the Spirit of God. Christian life is a matter of living out the life of the Spirit within them, which they have received from God as a gift. Possession of the Spirit is both a state of being and a norm for living. For this reason Paul can speak of the law of the Spirit of life in Rom 8:2.

3. Keeping the Law of Christ

In 1 Cor 9:19–22 Paul says that he has become all things to all people in order to save some of them. One example of this is that for those without the law, Paul has become like one without the law, even though he himself is not without the law of God but is in the law of Christ.[9]

> To those outside the law I became as one outside the law (though I am not free from God's law but am under Christ's law) so that I might win those outside the law. (1 Cor 9:21)

Similarly, in Gal 6:2 Paul suggests that the Galatians should fulfill the law of Christ.

What is the law of Christ? One possibility is that it refers to the teaching of Christ. If this is what Paul means, he is probably referring to Jesus' identification of the commandments to love God and neighbor as the two greatest commandments in Mark 12:28–34 and parallels. He might particularly have in mind Jesus' statement in Matt 22:40 that the whole law hangs on these two commandments. In Gal 6:2 Paul states that the Galatians will fulfill the law of Christ by bearing one another's burdens, which is equivalent to

---

9. On the law of Christ, see Bultmann, *Theology of the New Testament*, 1:343–44; Furnish, *Theology and Ethics*, 59–65; Dunn, *Theology of Paul*, 649–58.

loving one's neighbor. A few verses earlier (in 5:14) Paul had said that the whole law is summed up in the commandment to love one's neighbor (cf. Rom 13:8–10).

Whether or not Paul understands the law of Christ as a reference to Jesus' teaching about the two great commandments, it is fairly clear that the law of Christ is the law of love that sums up the Mosaic law. This shows us again that, for Paul, the law is problematic not because of its content but because it could not save the human race from slavery to sin and death. It had another role in salvation history and so does not serve as a norm for Gentile Christian behavior. When Christians are incorporated into Christ and live in a way appropriate to that new situation, however, they love one another and so fulfill the law of Christ, which is the law of God.

4. Imitation of Christ

In 1 Cor 11:1 Paul urges the Corinthians to be imitators of him as he imitates Christ.[10]

Be imitators of me, as I am of Christ.

In 1 Thess 1:6 Paul says that the Thessalonians have become imitators of him and his coworkers and of the Lord. In Rom 15:7 Paul urges the Romans to welcome one another as Christ has welcomed them. And in Phil 2:5 he urges the Philippians to have the same mind that was in Christ Jesus.

This should probably be understood as equivalent to incorporation into Christ, especially into his death and resurrection. In becoming part of the body of Christ and enacting this in their subsequent behavior, the behavior of Christians conforms to that of Christ. Thus they can be said to imitate him. The mind of Christ that Paul urges the Philippians to have is the mind Christ mani-

---

10. On the imitation of Christ, see Furnish, *Theology and Ethics*, 218–23. The idea that Jesus' followers should imitate him is also expressed by the saying of Jesus found in Matt 10:24–25a/Luke 6:40 (cf. John 13:16; 15:20), "A disciple is not above the teacher, nor a slave above the master; it is enough for the disciple to be like the teacher, and the slave like the master."

fested in emptying himself and humbling himself to the point of crucifixion before being exalted by God (Phil 2:6–11). The Thessalonians have imitated the Lord in receiving the word with joy despite persecution.

Content of Christian Life

According to Paul, Christian ethics is not basically a matter of a unique way of life. Rather, dying and rising with Christ make it possible for human beings to follow what is generally agreed to be a good way of living. For Paul, the human predicament is not ignorance of what constitutes proper behavior but the inability to do what one knows one ought. As slaves to sin and death, human beings know how they ought to behave but are unable to do so. Having been set free from this slavery through Christ, they can now live as they always knew they should.

For this reason, the way of life Paul recommends is very similar to that recommended by contemporary Jews and by many contemporary Gentiles.[11] Paul gives specifically Christian reasons for this way of life, but the behavior itself is not unique. This is especially true when he sets forth his ethical teaching generally, using standard forms for ethical teaching.

One such form is the list of vices and virtues, which Paul uses rather frequently.[12] Lists of vices are found in many places, including Rom 1:29–31.[13]

29 They were filled with every kind of wickedness, evil, covetousness, malice. Full of envy, murder, strife, deceit, craftiness, they are gossips, 30 slanderers, God-haters, insolent, haughty, boastful, inventors of evil, rebellious toward parents, 31 foolish, faithless, heartless, ruthless.

---

11. See Dunn, *Theology of Paul*, 661–67.

12. See Furnish, *Theology and Ethics*, 84–89; Fitzmyer, *Paul and His Theology*, 101; Dunn, *Theology of Paul*, 662–64.

13. See Rom 1:29–31; 13:13; 1 Cor 5:10–11; 6:9–10; 2 Cor 12:20; Gal 5:19–21; Eph 5:3–5; Col 3:5, 8.

Lists of virtues also occur in many places, including 2 Cor 6:6–7.[14] In this passage Paul says that he commends himself

> 6 by purity, knowledge, patience, kindness, holiness of spirit, genuine love, 7 truthful speech, and the power of God.

These lists are similar to those found in Hellenistic philosophical writings and Palestinian Jewish texts, in both form and content. Paul, however, gives specifically Christian motivations for these behaviors, as when he presents the virtues of Gal 5:22–23 as the fruit of the Spirit.

Another standard form for ethical teaching is the *Haustafel* (plural, *Haustafeln*), or table of household rules.[15] We find examples of this form in Col 3:18—4:1 and Eph 5:22—6:9.[16] In these passages ethical advice is given in turn to wives, husbands, children, fathers, slaves, and masters. The advice given to each is not specifically Christian, but Paul does give a specifically Christian motivation for the behavior recommended. For example, Col 3:18 says,

> Wives, be subject to your husbands, as is fitting in the Lord.

The idea that wives should be subject to their husbands is not specifically Christian, but the idea that they should do so because it is fitting in the Lord is specifically Christian.

In Rom 2:14–15 Paul speaks of Gentiles as doing by nature what the law requires and having the work of the law written on their hearts.

> 14 When Gentiles, who do not possess the law, do instinctively what the law requires, these, though not having the law, are a law to themselves. 15 They show that what the law requires is written on their hearts, to which their own conscience also bears witness.

These expressions approach, but perhaps fall short of, the idea of natural law as a norm for human behavior. In this same passage,

---

14. See 2 Cor 6:6–7; Gal 5:22–23; Phil 4:8; Col 3:12.

15. See Fitzmyer, *Paul and His Theology*, 101; Dunn, *Theology of Paul*, 666–67.

16. Cf. also Titus 2:2–10 and, outside the Pauline corpus, 1 Peter 2:18–3:7.

Paul says that the conscience of Gentiles bears witness to this law.[17] As we have noted when discussing this passage in "Humanity apart from Christ," Paul seems to regard the Gentiles' keeping the law in this way as an unrealized possibility, since he says that all humans have sinned. Perhaps Paul thinks that those incorporated into Christ can follow the natural law. If so, he does not say this explicitly.

Paul approaches the idea of natural law only in Rom 2:14–15. But he speaks about conscience in other passages in addition to this one, apparently adopting the idea from popular Hellenistic philosophy. In Rom 9:1 (cf. 2 Cor 1:12) he says that his conscience testifies to the truth of what he says. He speaks about conscience as a guide for behavior in Rom 13:5 and 1 Cor 10:25, 27.[18] In 2 Cor 4:2; 5:11 Paul also mentions the importance of the way other's consciences judge him.

All of this is similar to the way other moral teachers of Paul's day speak about conscience. Confronted by divisions within the Corinthian church, however, Paul develops the last point in a specifically Christian way. In 1 Cor 8:7–12; 10:28–29 Paul argues that there is need to adapt one's behavior to the consciences of other Christians. The first of these passages reads,

> 7 It is not everyone, however, who has this knowledge. Since some have become so accustomed to idols until now, they still think of the food they eat as food offered to an idol; and their conscience, being weak, is defiled. 8 "Food will not bring us close to God." We are no worse off if we do not eat, and no better off if we do. 9 But take care that this liberty of yours does not somehow become a stumbling block to the weak. 10 For if others see you, who possess knowledge, eating in the temple of an idol, might they not, since their conscience is weak, be encouraged to the point of eating food sacrificed to idols? 11 So by your knowledge those weak believers for whom Christ died are destroyed. 12 But when you thus sin

---

17. On natural law and conscience in Paul, see Fitzmyer, *Paul and His Theology*, 101–3.

18. Cf. also 1 Tim 1:5, 19; 3:9; 4:2; 2 Tim 1:3; Titus 1:15.

against members of your family, and wound their conscience when it is weak, you sin against Christ.

Paul does not mean that the conscience of other Christians should determine one's own conscience. But at least in some instances, one should not act in accord with one's own conscience if it would cause problems for the conscience of other Christians. This is true even if their conscience is defective. The reason for this is that Christ died for these believers (1 Cor 8:11); any sin against them is a sin against Christ (v. 12) because they are incorporated into Christ. Therefore one should sacrifice the freedom to follow one's own conscience for their sake. This is a specifically Christian ethical position.

There are other examples of such specifically Christian behavior in Paul's ethical teaching. Paul seems to recommend such behavior when he is not giving general ethical instruction but is reflecting on particular situations in order to see what behavior is appropriate for Christians. When Paul considers how the indicative leads to the imperative in a negative sense, his ethical teaching tends not to be distinctively Christian.

One outstanding exception to this is Paul's argument that Gentile Christians should not keep the Jewish law. This is a distinctively Christian ethical position that emerges from consideration of how the indicative leads to the imperative in a negative sense. As we have seen above in "Humanity apart from Christ," "Salvation as a Free Gift," "The Action of Christ," and "Salvation as Death with Christ to Sin," Paul understood the law as part of the bondage to sin from which Christ freed people. Paul affirmed the divine origin and essential goodness of the law. Therefore he argued that the involvement of the law in the enslavement of the human race to sin was intended by God as part of the divine plan of salvation. The specific role played by the law in the plan of salvation, however, means that for Gentile Christians to keep the law is a negation of their salvation in Christ. It would be a return to the slavery to sin from which Christ has saved them.

Distinctively Christian ethical teaching tends to emerge most of all when Paul explores the positive way the indicative leads to the imperative. We will consider two additional examples of Paul's distinctively Christian ethical teaching. Another example will emerge from our discussion of Romans 12–15.

1. Relationship between Husbands and Wives

As we have just noted, Paul's advice to husbands and wives in the *Haustafeln* is rather conventional, though given a specifically Christian foundation. Likewise, in 1 Cor 14:33b–35 Paul says that women should be silent in the assemblies and subordinate and should ask their husbands at home anything they want to know.

> 33b As in all the churches of the saints, 34 women should be silent in the churches. For they are not permitted to speak, but should be subordinate, as the law also says. 35 If there is anything they desire to know, let them ask their husbands at home. For it is shameful for a woman to speak in church.

This is also conventional, as Paul himself suggests by saying that this is done in all the assemblies of the saints (v. 33b) and that it is shameful for a woman to speak in the assembly (v. 35).[19]

In 1 Cor 7:1–16, 28, 32–34, however, Paul carefully takes up the case of both husband and wife in parallel sentences throughout the argument, suggesting a radical equality between spouses.[20] This is not conventional but arises from reflection on the implications of having died and risen with Christ. In general it can be seen as flowing from the negation of formerly meaningful distinctions through baptism into Christ as expressed in Gal 3:28 (see "Baptism," above).

In 1 Cor 7:1–16 Paul responds to the Corinthians' statement "It is well for a man not to touch a woman" (v. 1).

> 1 Now concerning the matters about which you wrote: "It is well for a man not to touch a woman." 2 But because of cases of sexual immorality, each man should have his own wife and each woman her own husband. 3 The husband should give to his wife her conjugal rights, and likewise the wife to her hus-

---

19. R. F. Collins argues that in vv. 33b–35 Paul quotes a statement of the Corinthians that he rejects in v. 36 (*First Corinthians*, 514–15, 517).

20. See Fitzmyer, *Paul and His Theology*, 104–5; Dunn, *Theology of Paul*, 692–98.

band. 4 For the wife does not have authority over her own
body, but the husband does; likewise the husband does not
have authority over his own body, but the wife does. 5 Do not
deprive one another except perhaps by agreement for a set
time, to devote yourselves to prayer, and then come together
again, so that Satan may not tempt you because of your lack of
self-control. 6 This I say by way of concession, not of command. 7 I wish that all were as I myself am. But each has a particular gift from God, one having one kind and another a
different kind.

Paul does not reject the Corinthians' assertion but modifies it in
significant ways. In verses 2–7 he says that this view should not
cause married couples to cease having sexual intercourse with one
another. Husbands and wives should have sexual intercourse with
one another (v. 2) and should give one another their conjugal rights
(v. 3). "For the wife does not have authority over her own body, but
the husband does; likewise, the husband does not have authority
over his own body, but the wife does" (v. 4). At most, spouses should
cease sexual relations for a limited time, by mutual agreement, to
devote themselves to prayer (v. 5). The view that husbands and
wives have authority over one another's bodies may be based on the
idea that sexual relations unite husband and wife into one body (see
"Sex and Marriage," above).

In verse 7 Paul says that he wishes all were as he himself is
(i.e., unmarried; cf. v. 8) but each person has a particular charism
from God. Paul sympathizes with the desire of the married
Corinthians to cease sexual relations but implies that they have not
received the charism of doing so whereas he has. The idea that
marriage and celibacy are charisms may be based on Paul's view
that Christians receive different gifts from the Holy Spirit that
together form the body of Christ (see "Church," above).

In verses 10–12 Paul says that the wife should not separate
from her husband and the husband should not divorce his wife.

10 To the married I give this command—not I but the Lord—
that the wife should not separate from her husband 11 (but if
she does separate, let her remain unmarried or else be reconciled to her husband), and that the husband should not divorce

his wife. 12 To the rest I say—I and not the Lord—that if any believer has a wife who is an unbeliever, and she consents to live with him, he should not divorce her.

This is explicitly based on the teaching of Jesus (v. 10). This teaching is found in Mark 10:2–12 and elsewhere.[21]

In verses 13–16 Paul discusses the case of marriage between a Christian and a non-Christian, apparently seeing this as something not addressed by the teaching of Jesus (cf. v. 12).

13 And if any woman has a husband who is an unbeliever, and he consents to live with her, she should not divorce him. 14 For the unbelieving husband is made holy through his wife, and the unbelieving wife is made holy through her husband. Otherwise, your children would be unclean, but as it is, they are holy. 15 But if the unbelieving partner separates, let it be so; in such a case the brother or sister is not bound. It is to peace that God has called you. 16 Wife, for all you know, you might save your husband. Husband, for all you know, you might save your wife.

Husbands and wives having a non-Christian spouse should not divorce them as long as the non-Christian spouse is willing to remain married to the Christian partner (v. 12–13), because the non-Christian partner is made holy through the Christian spouse (v. 14; cf. v. 16). If the non-Christian partner separates, however, the Christian husband or wife is not bound (v. 15).

First Corinthians 7:28, 32–34 is part of Paul's discussion of a distinct but related topic, namely, virgins (cf. v. 25).

28 But if you marry, you do not sin, and if a virgin marries, she does not sin. Yet those who marry will experience distress in this life, and I would spare you that.... 32 I want you to be free from anxieties. The unmarried man is anxious about the affairs of the Lord, how to please the Lord; 33 but the married man is anxious about the affairs of the world, how to please his wife, 34 and his interests are divided. And the unmarried woman and the virgin are anxious about the affairs of the Lord, so that

21. See Matt 5:31–32; 19:3–9; Luke 16:18.

they may be holy in body and spirit; but the married woman is anxious about the affairs of the world, how to please her husband.

In the course of this discussion, Paul says that if "you" (presumably a male) marry, you do not sin and if a virgin marries, she does not sin (v. 28). It is advantageous, however, not to marry because the unmarried man or woman is anxious about the affairs of the Lord but the married man or woman is anxious about how to please his or her spouse (vv. 32–34).

Throughout this discussion, Paul seems to take great care to show the equality of husband and wife in every way. Most striking is the statement in verse 4 that husbands and wives have authority over one another's bodies. Perhaps Paul needed to safeguard the interests of Christian women in these matters.

2. Slavery

We have noted above that Paul's advice to masters and slaves in the *Haustafeln* is conventional though given a specifically Christian foundation. Likewise, in 1 Cor 7:21–24 Paul's advice that slaves not seek freedom is not specifically Christian though supported by Christian arguments.

When Paul discusses the case of the slave Onesimus in his letter to Philemon, however, he makes some specifically Christian recommendations.[22]

10 I am appealing to you for my child, Onesimus, whose father I have become during my imprisonment. 11 Formerly he was useless to you, but now he is indeed useful both to you and to me. 12 I am sending him, that is, my own heart, back to you. 13 I wanted to keep him with me, so that he might be of service to me in your place during my imprisonment for the gospel; 14 but I preferred to do nothing without your consent, in order that your good deed might be voluntary and not something forced. 15 Perhaps this is the reason he was separated from you for a while, so that you might have him back

---

22. See Fitzmyer, *Paul and His Theology*, 106–7; Dunn, *Theology of Paul*, 698–701.

forever, 16 no longer as a slave but more than a slave, a beloved brother—especially to me but how much more to you, both in the flesh and in the Lord. 17 So if you consider me your partner, welcome him as you would welcome me. 18 If he has wronged you in any way, or owes you anything, charge that to my account. 19 I, Paul, am writing this with my own hand: I will repay it. I say nothing about your owing me even your own self.

Onesimus was apparently a slave belonging to Philemon (v. 16) who had run away from Philemon. He had come into contact with Paul and through Paul become a Christian; in this way Paul became his father (v. 10). Paul is sending Onesimus back to Philemon (v. 12) with this letter. In returning Onesimus, Paul complies with Roman law that required the return of runaway slaves.

The purpose of the letter is to appeal to Philemon on behalf of Onesimus (v. 10). Paul says that he could command Philemon but prefers to appeal to him on the basis of love (vv. 8–9). Paul clearly asks Philemon to welcome Onesimus as he would welcome Paul (v. 17). If Onesimus has wronged Philemon or owes him anything, Philemon should charge that to Paul's account, and Paul will repay it. Of course, Paul has a very large credit in his account with Philemon because Philemon owes Paul his very self (vv. 18–19). Paul also seems to suggest strongly that Philemon should send Onesimus back to Paul. In verses 13–14 Paul says that he wanted to keep Onesimus with him but did not want to do so without Philemon's consent so that the good deed of allowing Onesimus to remain with Paul might not be forced on Philemon.

In all of this Paul raises no fundamental question about slavery as an institution. Onesimus's conversion to Christianity, however, implies modification of the institution. Because Onesimus is a Christian and under the sponsorship of Paul, Philemon should not punish him as would be his legal right. Onesimus is now more than a slave; he is a beloved brother of both Paul and Philemon (v. 16). Paul also suggests returning Onesimus to Paul in order to serve Paul on behalf of Philemon. Although this need not imply that Philemon free Onesimus, it does mean that effectively Onesimus would not be a slave at Philemon's disposal during the time he was with Paul. In these ways Christianity undermines the institution of slavery in this case.

In general Paul sees Christian life as what all agree to be a good way of life. But a more specifically Christian ethic emerges as Paul reflects on particular ethical questions in light of dying and rising with Christ. This suggests an avenue for further development of Christian ethics. Such development has clearly occurred with respect to slavery. Christians now would say that slavery is incompatible with Christian faith. This view is in continuity with the trend of Paul's thinking about this subject but goes far beyond it.

Romans 12:1—15:13

Romans 12:1—15:13 is the exhortation section of the letter to the Romans. Here Paul offers ethical advice to the Roman Christians. In 12:1—13:14 he offers general ethical instruction, recommending behavior that is also recommended by contemporary Jews and Gentiles; one of his lists of vices occurs in 13:13. Paul gives Christian reasons for this behavior and occasionally recommends specifically Christian behavior. In 14:1—15:13 he recommends distinctively Christian behavior as he reflects on a particular issue confronting the Roman Christians.

In 12:1–2 Paul states the theme of his exhortation.

> 1 I appeal to you therefore, brothers and sisters, by the mercies of God, to present your bodies as a living sacrifice, holy and acceptable to God, which is your spiritual worship. 2 Do not be conformed to this world, but be transformed by the renewing of your minds, so that you may discern what is the will of God—what is good and acceptable and perfect.

Paul asks the Roman Christians to present themselves as a living sacrifice to God, not being conformed to this world but transformed by the renewal of their minds.

In verses 3–8 Paul specifies this as meaning not thinking of oneself more highly than one ought. This behavior is not specifically Christian, but Paul argues for it on the basis of his understanding of the church as the body of Christ (see "Church," above).

In verses 9–13 Paul continues to specify Christian life as consisting of various behaviors, such as genuine love, hating what is evil, and so on. Paul lists more generally good behavior in verses 14–21. Examples include living in harmony and not being haughty (v. 16).

> 14 Bless those who persecute you; bless and do not curse them. 15 Rejoice with those who rejoice, weep with those who weep. 16 Live in harmony with one another; do not be haughty, but associate with the lowly; do not claim to be wiser than you are. 17 Do not repay anyone evil for evil, but take thought for what is noble in the sight of all. 18 If it is possible, so far as it depends on you, live peaceably with all. 19 Beloved, never avenge yourselves, but leave room for the wrath of God; for it is written, "Vengeance is mine, I will repay, says the Lord." 20 No, "if your enemies are hungry, feed them; if they are thirsty, give them something to drink; for by doing this you will heap burning coals on their heads." 21 Do not be overcome by evil, but overcome evil with good.

The main theme of verses 14–21 is that Christians should bless those who persecute them (v. 14), not repay evil for evil (v. 17), leave vengeance to God (vv. 19–20), and overcome evil with good (v. 21). The third of these is explicitly based on two scriptural passages that Paul quotes, namely, Deut 32:35 and Prov 25:21–22. To this extent the behavior Paul recommends here can be seen as that recommended by the Jewish tradition.

In 13:1–7 Paul urges the Roman Christians to be subject to the governing authorities.

> 1 Let every person be subject to the governing authorities; for there is no authority except from God, and those authorities that exist have been instituted by God. 2 Therefore whoever resists authority resists what God has appointed, and those who resist will incur judgment. 3 For rulers are not a terror to good conduct, but to bad. Do you wish to have no fear of the

authority? Then do what is good, and you will receive its approval; 4 for it is God's servant for your good. But if you do what is wrong, you should be afraid, for the authority does not bear the sword in vain! It is the servant of God to execute wrath on the wrongdoer. 5 Therefore one must be subject, not only because of wrath but also because of conscience. 6 For the same reason you also pay taxes, for the authorities are God's servants, busy with this very thing. 7 Pay to all what is due them—taxes to whom taxes are due, revenue to whom revenue is due, respect to whom respect is due, honor to whom honor is due.

This behavior does not differ from that recommended by many other moral teachers. Paul argues that the governing authorities should be obeyed because God has established them (see vv. 1–2, 4–6). Paul may make this point in response to recent disturbances in Rome, but does not say so explicitly. The emperor Claudius had expelled Jews from Rome in 49 CE. They may have been allowed to return shortly before Paul wrote to the Romans.

In 13:8–10 Paul again urges those he addresses to love one another.

8 Owe no one anything, except to love one another; for the one who loves another has fulfilled the law. 9 The commandments, "You shall not commit adultery; You shall not murder; You shall not steal; You shall not covet"; and any other commandment, are summed up in this word, "Love your neighbor as yourself." 10 Love does no wrong to a neighbor; therefore, love is the fulfilling of the law.

In this case he argues that love is the fulfillment of the Jewish law (vv. 8, 10). All other commandments are summed up in the command "Love your neighbor as yourself" (Lev 19:18) (v. 9).

Paul ends the first part of the exhortation section in 13:11–14 by urging the Roman Christians to behave in the ways he has urged because they know that the end is at hand.

11 Besides this, you know what time it is, how it is now the moment for you to wake from sleep. For salvation is nearer to us now than when we became believers; 12 the night is far

> gone, the day is near. Let us then lay aside the works of dark-
> ness and put on the armor of light; 13 let us live honorably as
> in the day, not in reveling and drunkenness, not in debauchery
> and licentiousness, not in quarreling and jealousy. 14 Instead,
> put on the Lord Jesus Christ, and make no provision for the
> flesh, to gratify its desires.

They should live as is appropriate for the new day that is about to
dawn (v. 13). This is a basis for behavior that Christians shared with
Jews who thought the end of the world was near. But Paul ends by
telling them to put on Christ (v. 14). As we have seen in "Humanity
in Christ," putting on Christ is an expression of Paul's basic understanding of Christian existence as union with Christ. Here he uses
the idea as the basis for behavior. Implicitly he says, "You are united
with Christ; continue in that union by living appropriately."

In 14:1–15:13 Paul discusses the relationship between those
Paul calls "weak in faith" (14:1) and those he calls "strong," with
whom Paul identifies himself (15:1). He appeals to the strong to welcome the weak and supports this by arguing that neither should
judge the other. This is similar to the argument Paul makes in 1 Cor
8:1–11:1. Some interpreters have seen the discussion in Romans as a
generalization of the teaching presented in 1 Corinthians. But it is
more likely that Paul is addressing an issue confronting the Roman
Christians and about which Paul has heard. Perhaps when Claudius
expelled Jews from Rome in 49, most of the Jewish Christians were
expelled along with them, leaving the Christian community in
Rome largely a Gentile community. When the Jews were allowed
to return to Rome several years later, Jewish Christians rejoined the
church in Rome. They were not welcomed by the Gentile
Christians who had never left Rome, and the two groups had diffi-
culty reuniting.[23]

In this interpretation, the "weak in faith" are Jewish
Christians. Paul says that they eat only vegetables (Rom 14:2, 21),
judge one day to be better than another (v. 5), and avoid drinking
wine (v. 21). Eating vegetables can be seen as motivated by the
desire to avoid eating unclean meat (cf. 14:14, 20), that is, meat that

---

23. For this interpretation, see Dunn, *Theology of Paul*, 680–89.

does not satisfy the requirements of the law. Both eating vegetables and abstaining from wine may have been motivated by the desire to avoid food or drink that had been offered to idols. And judging one day to be better than another may refer to Jewish observance of the Sabbath and other holy days. The "strong" are Gentile Christians who do none of these things.

Paul urges the strong to welcome the weak (14:1) and supports this in verses 3–12 by arguing that neither group should judge the other.

> 1 Welcome those who are weak in faith, but not for the purpose of quarreling over opinions. 2 Some believe in eating anything, while the weak eat only vegetables. 3 Those who eat must not despise those who abstain, and those who abstain must not pass judgment on those who eat; for God has welcomed them. 4 Who are you to pass judgment on servants of another? It is before their own lord that they stand or fall. And they will be upheld, for the Lord is able to make them stand.... 7 We do not live to ourselves, and we do not die to ourselves. 8 If we live, we live to the Lord, and if we die, we die to the Lord; so then, whether we live or whether we die, we are the Lord's. 9 For to this end Christ died and lived again, so that he might be Lord of both the dead and the living. 10 Why do you pass judgment on your brother or sister? Or you, why do you despise your brother or sister? For we will all stand before the judgment seat of God. 11 For it is written, "As I live, says the Lord, every knee shall bow to me, and every tongue shall give praise to God." 12 So then, each of us will be accountable to God.

They should not judge one another because God has welcomed both groups (v. 3) and both are servants of God (vv. 4, 7–9), to whom they will be accountable (vv. 10–12).

In 14:13–23 Paul urges the strong not to put an obstacle in the way of the weak.

> 13 Let us therefore no longer pass judgment on one another, but resolve instead never to put a stumbling block or hindrance in the way of another. 14 I know and am persuaded in the Lord Jesus that nothing is unclean in itself; but it is unclean

for anyone who thinks it unclean. 15 If your brother or sister is being injured by what you eat, you are no longer walking in love. Do not let what you eat cause the ruin of one for whom Christ died. 16 So do not let your good be spoken of as evil. 17 For the kingdom of God is not food and drink but righteousness and peace and joy in the Holy Spirit. 18 The one who thus serves Christ is acceptable to God and has human approval. 19 Let us then pursue what makes for peace and for mutual upbuilding. 20 Do not, for the sake of food, destroy the work of God. Everything is indeed clean, but it is wrong for you to make others fall by what you eat; 21 it is good not to eat meat or drink wine or do anything that makes your brother or sister stumble. 22 The faith that you have, have as your own conviction before God. Blessed are those who have no reason to condemn themselves because of what they approve. 23 But those who have doubts are condemned if they eat, because they do not act from faith; for whatever does not proceed from faith is sin.

The behavior of the strong could cause problems for the weak in two ways. First, it could cause the weak to condemn the strong as behaving wrongly (v. 16). Second and more important, it could cause the weak to imitate the behavior of the strong, doing things the weak regard as wrong (vv. 20, 23). Even though the behavior of the strong is not improper (vv. 14, 20), they should avoid it in order to avoid injuring the weak. The strong should not let what they eat cause the ruin of one for whom Christ died (v. 15). Instead they should do what makes for peace and mutual upbuilding (v. 19). "The kingdom of God is not food and drink but righteousness and peace and joy in the Holy Spirit" (v. 17).

In 15:1–6 Paul says that the strong should put up with the failings of the weak and not please themselves.

1 We who are strong ought to put up with the failings of the weak, and not to please ourselves. 2 Each of us must please our neighbor for the good purpose of building up the neighbor. 3 For Christ did not please himself; but, as it is written, "The insults of those who insult you have fallen on me." 4 For whatever was written in former days was written for our instruction, so that by steadfastness and by the encouragement of the

171

scriptures we might have hope. 5 May the God of steadfastness and encouragement grant you to live in harmony with one another, in accordance with Christ Jesus, 6 so that together you may with one voice glorify the God and Father of our Lord Jesus Christ.

They should not please themselves because this is how Christ acted (v. 3). Paul ends with a prayer that the Roman Christians will live in harmony in accordance with Christ Jesus (vv. 5–6).

Paul ends the discussion of this topic in 15:7–13 by urging strong and weak to welcome one another as Christ welcomed them. Christ became a servant of the circumcised (v. 8) in order that Gentiles might glorify God (vv. 9–12). Like Christ, the strong should serve the weak, and the weak should recognize that inclusion of the Gentiles was the ultimate goal of God's salvation.

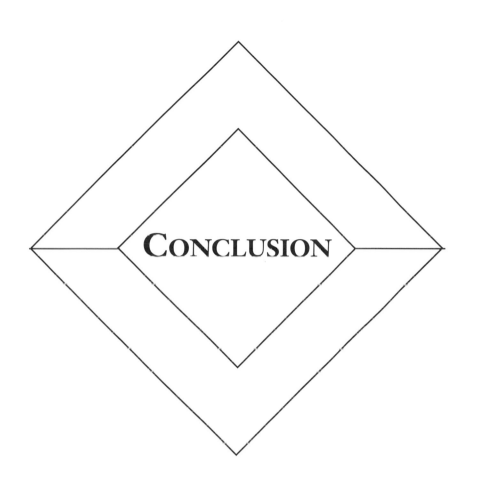

CONCLUSION

In the foregoing we have discussed in some detail the theological system that can be derived from the letters of Paul. In doing so, we have seen, sometimes explicitly, more often implicitly, that this theological system is not identical with the beliefs of Christians today. This is not surprising. The letters of Paul are only one part of the New Testament, and the New Testament is only the beginning of what has so far been almost two millennia of reflection on the meaning of Jesus Christ. When the letters of Paul are combined with the rest of the New Testament, the result is different from any part of the New Testament alone. As the church has deepened its understanding of Jesus through the centuries, under the guidance of the Holy Spirit, new insights have been added to those contained in the New Testament.

Still, despite the propriety of combining the letters of Paul with the rest of the New Testament, and of continued theological reflection on the New Testament, in this process valuable ideas have been lost to view. Retrieval of such ideas would enrich current Christian belief. This chapter discusses several of Paul's ideas that it would be helpful to retrieve. It will try to show what retrieving them might mean by contrasting them with the summary of Christian belief contained in the *Catechism of the Catholic Church*. These are only examples of ideas it would be helpful to retrieve, but they are the most important examples.

1. Humanity apart from Christ

This topic is treated in the *Catechism* under the headings "Body and Soul but Truly One" (§§ 362–68) and "Original Sin" (§§ 396–409). The former discusses anthropology, and the latter, sin.

In discussing Paul's anthropology above, we noted differences between it and what was referred to as "our anthropology." The latter is reflected in the *Catechism*, most clearly in its affirmation of the immortality of the soul (§ 366). In line with this, the *Catechism* gives the terms "body" (§ 362), "soul" (§ 363), and "spirit" (§ 367) different meanings than does Paul. On the other hand, the *Catechism* and Paul agree in emphasizing the unity of the human being (see §§ 364–65) and give the term "heart" a similar meaning (§ 368).

In order to understand the letters of Paul, it is clearly necessary to understand his anthropology. This is particularly the case with regard to the special meaning he gives the word "flesh." It would be valuable for Christians today to retrieve Paul's anthropology for themselves; doing so would mean replacing a dualistic understanding of human nature with a more integral one. This would be difficult, however, because a dualistic anthropology is so deeply embedded in our culture. Fortunately, other ideas of Paul can be retrieved without retrieving Paul's anthropology. Paul's ideas are based on his anthropology, but they can be adapted to the different anthropology now embodied in the *Catechism*.

The teaching of the *Catechism* with regard to sin is closer to that of Paul; nevertheless, Paul has some ideas about sin that would be good to retrieve. The *Catechism* and Paul agree in seeing sin as idolatry (§ 398) and transgression of law (§§ 396–97). Paul, however, thinks mainly of transgression of the Jewish law, whereas the *Catechism* speaks of the laws of creation and the moral norms (§ 396). The *Catechism* and Paul also agree in seeing death as a consequence of sin (§ 400), seeing sin as having other cosmic consequences (§ 400), and seeing the origin of sin in the sin of Adam, which affected the entire human race (§§ 402–3).

The *Catechism* says nothing about Paul's idea that God gave the law to Israel in order to bring sin to light. And the *Catechism* goes beyond Paul in saying that, as a consequence of sin,

> the control of the soul's spiritual faculties over the body is shattered. (§ 400)

> Human nature...is wounded in the natural powers proper to it; subject to ignorance, suffering, and the dominion of death; and inclined to sin—an inclination to evil that is called "concupiscence." (§ 405, cf. § 1264)

It also goes beyond Paul in saying that Adam and Eve transmitted this fallen human nature by means of propagation (§ 404).

As we have seen, Paul speaks of slavery to sin and death rather than fallen human nature. The latter can certainly be seen as a helpful development and specification of the former. It seems especially compatible with the idea that death is a consequence of sin, which may imply some change in human nature itself. On the other hand, the idea that human nature is fallen severely limits the extent to which salvation can be understood as realized here and now.

Paul does not think that salvation is completely realized at present; Christians are freed from slavery to sin but remain subject to death. Paul never explains more fully his precise understanding of this intermediate situation, perhaps because he did not expect it to last very long. But Paul's understanding of original sin as having led to enslavement rather than to a change in human nature allows for salvation to be rather fully realized at the present time. One can be released from slavery now, but fallen human nature will be restored to its original condition only at the end of time. It might be helpful to retrieve Paul's idea that apart from Christ, human beings are enslaved to sin and that Christ releases them from this slavery.

The idea that the sin of Adam was transmitted by propagation helpfully explains how that sin affected others. On the other hand, it becomes problematic if the human race did not literally descend from one man and woman who sinned. And some ways of understanding this transmission imply a negative view of sexual intercourse. Paul's less specific understanding of the way Adam's sin affected the whole human race avoids these problems and may be valuable to retrieve for that reason. This would be compatible with the *Catechism's* statement that the transmission of original sin is a mystery we cannot fully understand (§ 404).

It would be valuable to retrieve Paul's understanding of the purpose of the law because it is part of the way he explains why Gentile Christians are not bound to keep the biblical law. They do not keep the law but often cannot explain why. It would be good for them to be able to do so.

2. The Action of Christ (Soteriology)

This topic is treated in the *Catechism* under the headings "Christ's Redemptive Death in God's Plan of Salvation" (§§ 599–605), "Christ Offered Himself to His Father for Our Sins" (§§ 606–18), and "On the Third Day He Rose from the Dead" (§§ 638–55).

The *Catechism* and Paul agree in saying that the death of Jesus (§ 601) and his resurrection (§§ 638, 654) together constitute the means by which Jesus is Savior. They also agree in understanding Jesus' death as a sacrifice (§§ 608, 613–14) and as vicarious (§ 615).

The *Catechism* speaks of union with Christ in death (§ 618) and resurrection (§§ 655, 1002–3) but in a somewhat different way than Paul does. According to the *Catechism*, participation in the paschal mystery is offered to all because Christ has united himself to all people through his incarnation. It then goes on to speak about imitating the example of Christ. The *Catechism* hints at union with Christ in death as a means of salvation but does not express this idea clearly. In speaking of resurrection the *Catechism* emphasizes that Christ's resurrection is the assurance of the future resurrection of Christians. But it also mentions that Christians "are swept up by Christ into the heart of divine life" (§ 655).

The *Catechism* goes beyond Paul when it integrates incarnation into what it says about union with Christ in death. In a similar way, it goes beyond Paul by integrating incarnation into its understanding of Christ's death as a sacrifice (§ 614) and by saying that Christ's resurrection confirmed his works and teaching (§ 651) and his divinity (§ 653). On the other hand, the *Catechism* says nothing about Paul's idea that salvation through the cross of Christ is a scandal.

It would be valuable to retrieve the idea of the cross as a scandal because it is the basis on which Paul argues that the ways of God are different from human ways. It is possible, however, to come to this same view in other ways.

It would be very valuable to retrieve Paul's idea that Christ's death and resurrection are salvific through Christians' participation in them. We have noted above (in "The Action of Christ") the two main ways in which this understanding of how Christ saves is superior to others: it gives saving significance to the resurrection of Jesus as well as his death, and it explains how the death and resurrection of Jesus not only saves Christians from sin but is also the means by which they enter into new life with Christ. Although the *Catechism* explicitly says that Jesus' resurrection is a saving event (§§ 651–55), it treats it separately from the death of Jesus. This is one indication that it does not understand the death and resurrection of Jesus as a unified salvific action in the way Paul does.

It is not necessary to choose a single explanation of the way Christ's death and resurrection are salvific; Paul himself does not do so. But it would be helpful to retrieve Paul's central idea—union with Jesus in death and resurrection—as that of Christians today.

3. Humanity in Christ

This topic is treated in the *Catechism* under the headings "The Church—Body of Christ" (§§ 787–96), "Baptism in the Church" (§§ 1226–28), "The Grace of Baptism" (§§ 1262–74), "The Paschal Banquet" (§§ 1382–1401), "Marriage in the Lord" (§§ 1612–17), and "The Love of Husband and Wife" (§§ 2360–65).

The *Catechism* speaks of the unity between believers and Christ (§§ 787–89), but it is not the *Catechism's* central conception of Christian life, as it is Paul's. Likewise the *Catechism* speaks of the union of believers and Christ as union with Christ in death and resurrection (§§ 790, 793) but does not emphasize this. It would be beneficial to accentuate these ideas as Paul does.

a) Baptism

Paul and the *Catechism* agree that baptism incorporates one into the body of Christ and that this union of believers with Christ also unites them to one another (§§ 1267, 1271–72, cf. 789). Paul and the *Catechism* also agree that baptism involves the Holy Spirit (§§ 1226–27, 1267), that in baptism one dies and rises with Christ (§§ 790, 1227), and that formerly meaningful distinctions are replaced by new distinctions (§§ 791, 1267). Paul speaks more about the negation of formerly meaningful distinctions than the *Catechism* does.

The *Catechism* connects baptism with faith, repentance, and forgiveness of sins (§§ 1226, 1263); Paul does not do this explicitly. The *Catechism* also goes beyond Paul in saying that baptism gives one a share in the common priesthood of all believers (§ 1268) and that baptism confers an indelible spiritual mark (§§ 1272–74).

b) Eucharist

Like Paul, the *Catechism* says that the Eucharist incorporates believers into the body of Christ (§ 1396), uniting them with Christ

(§§ 790, 1382, 1391) and one another (§§ 790, 1396). Although the *Catechism* emphasizes that the Eucharist is simultaneously the perpetuation of the sacrifice of the cross (§§ 1382–83, cf. 1393), it does not say explicitly that the union of Christians with Christ in the Eucharist is union with Christ in death and resurrection. Retrieval of this idea would relate these two aspects of the Eucharist more satisfactorily than the Catechism presently does.

Like Paul, the *Catechism* discusses proper participation in the Eucharist (§§ 1385–87). The *Catechism* does not, however, emphasize that this is a matter of discerning the presence of Christ in other Christians, as Paul does. The *Catechism* goes beyond Paul in speaking of the way the Eucharist separates Christians from sin (§§ 1393–95), commits them to the poor (§ 1397), and prompts them to work for the unity of all Christians (§ 1398).

c) Church

As we have noted in discussing baptism, the *Catechism* and Paul agree that the members of the church receive diverse gifts from the spirit. Both also agree that these gifts are mutually interdependent (§§ 791, 951). Paul, however, emphasizes this much more than the *Catechism* does. It would be beneficial to retrieve this idea as a central understanding of the church.

Paul and the *Catechism* agree that Christ is the head of the church (§§ 792–95). Unlike Paul, the *Catechism* speaks at some length about leadership of the church, though not in connection with the idea that the church is the body of Christ (see §§ 874–96).

d) Sex and Marriage

Paul and the *Catechism* agree in seeing an analogy between the relationship of Christ and the church in one body and the relationship created by sex and marriage between man and woman (§§ 796, 1616–17). Unlike Paul, the *Catechism* does not see the creation of such a relationship as intrinsic to sexual intercourse itself, whatever those involved may think they are doing. The *Catechism* does say, however, that sexual intercourse is intrinsically intended to create such a union (§§ 372, 2360–61).

Paul and the *Catechism* agree that within marriage sexual intercourse should create a relationship analogous to that of Christ and the church and that this analogy makes marriage a sign of the relationship between Christ and the church (§§ 1617, 2364–65).

As we can see, the *Catechism* presentation of baptism, Eucharist, church, and sex and marriage incorporates many of Paul's ideas about these subjects. It would be valuable, however, to retrieve dying and rising with Christ as the central significance of baptism and Eucharist, as they are for Paul. It would also be valuable to retrieve, as the central understanding of the church, the idea that the church is the body of Christ. Taking seriously Paul's view of the church as a living organism, that is, Christ himself, has the potential to change every aspect of church life. The *Catechism* presentation of sex and marriage is closest to that of Paul, but how fully is this view of sex and marriage operative among Christians today? It would be good to make it so.

Summary: Ideas of Paul Valuable to Retrieve

- The human being is a unity, not a duality
- Sin is enslavement
- The way Adam's sin affected the human race is not completely clear
- The purpose of the law was to increase sin as a preparation for the coming of salvation
- The cross is a scandal
- Christ's death and resurrection are salvific through Christians' participation in them
- Dying and rising with Christ is the central meaning of baptism and Eucharist
- The church is a living organism, the body of Christ
- Sex and marriage create a union between man and woman parallel to the union between Christ and the church

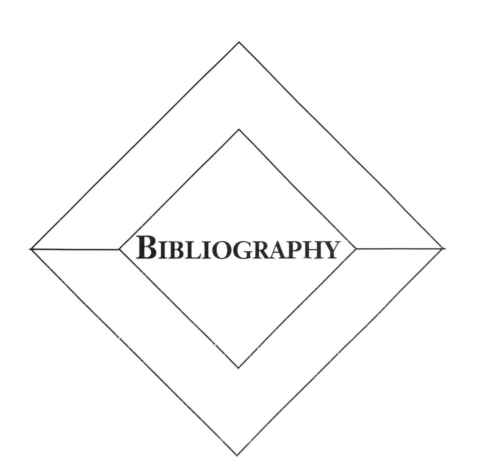

BIBLIOGRAPHY

Works Cited

Bassler, J. *Divine Impartiality: Paul and a Theological Axiom.* Society of Biblical Literature Dissertation Series 59. Chico, CA: Scholars, 1982.

Beker, J. C. *Paul the Apostle: The Triumph of God in Life and Thought.* Philadelphia: Fortress, 1980.

Best, Ernest. *One Body in Christ.* London: SPCK, 1955.

Bornkamm, G. *Paul.* Translated by D. M. G. Stalker. London: Hodder & Stoughton, 1971.

Bultmann, R. *Theology of the New Testament.* Vol. 1. Translated by K. Grobel. New York: Scribner, 1951.

Callan, T. *The Origins of Christian Faith.* New York/Mahwah, NJ: Paulist, 1994.

———. "Paul and the Golden Calf." *Proceedings of the Eastern Great Lakes and Midwest Biblical Societies* (1990): 1–17.

Collins, R. F. *First Corinthians.* Sacra pagina. Collegeville, MN: Liturgical Press, 1999.

Conzelmann, H. *An Outline of the Theology of the New Testament.* Translated by J. Bowden. New York and Evanston, IL: Harper & Row, 1969.

Dahl, N. A. "Form-Critical Observations on Early Christian Preaching." In *Jesus in the Memory of the Early Church*, 30–36. Minneapolis: Augsburg, 1976.

———. *Jesus the Christ: The Historical Origins of Christological Doctrine.* Minneapolis: Fortress, 1991.

Dibelius, M. "Die Christianisierung einer hellenistischen Formel." In *Botschaft und Geschichte*, 2:14–29. Tübingen: J. C. B. Mohr (Siebeck), 1956.

Dunn, J. D. G. *The Theology of Paul the Apostle.* Grand Rapids/Cambridge, Eng.: Eerdmans, 1998.

Fitzmyer, J. A. *Paul and His Theology: A Brief Sketch.* Englewood Cliffs, NJ: Prentice Hall, 1989.

———. "Pauline Teaching in Romans." In *Romans*, 103–43. Anchor Bible 33; New York: Doubleday, 1993.

185

Furnish, V. P. *The Moral Teaching of Paul: Selected Issues*. Nashville: Abingdon, 1985.

———. *Theology and Ethics in Paul*. Nashville/New York: Abingdon, 1968.

Gammie, J. G. *Holiness in Israel*. Overtures to Biblical Theology. Minneapolis: Fortress, 1989.

Gutierrez, P. *La paternité spirituelle selon saint Paul*. Études bibliques. Paris: Gabalda, 1968.

Hays, R. B. *The Faith of Jesus Christ: An Investigation of the Narrative Substructure of Galatians 3:1—4:11*. Society of Biblical Literature Dissertation Series 56. Chico, CA: Scholars, 1983.

Hengel, M. *The Son of God: The Origin of Christology and the History of Jewish-Hellenistic Religion*. Philadelphia: Fortress, 1976.

Kümmel, W. G. *Introduction to the New Testament*. Translated by H. C. Kee. Nashville: Abingdon, 1975.

Meeks, W. A. "'And Rose Up to Play': Midrash and Paraenesis in 1 Corinthians 10:1–22." *Journal for the Study of the New Testament* 16 (1982): 64–78.

———. *The First Urban Christians: The Social World of the Apostle Paul*. New Haven/London: Yale University Press, 1983.

———, ed., *The Writings of St. Paul*. New York: Norton, 1972.

Moore, G. F. *Judaism in the First Centuries of the Christian Era: the Age of the Tannaim*. New York: Schocken, 1971.

Murphy-O'Connor, J. *Paul: A Critical Life*. Oxford: Clarendon, 1996.

Norden, E. *Agnostos Theos*. Stuttgart: Teubner, 1956.

Ridderbos, H. *Paul: An Outline of His Theology*. Translated by J. R. de Witt. Grand Rapids: Eerdmans, 1975.

Robinson, J. A. T. *The Body: A Study in Pauline Theology*. London: SCM, 1952.

Sanders, E. P. *Paul and Palestinian Judaism: A Comparison of Patterns of Religion*. Philadelphia: Fortress, 1977.

Schoeps, H. J. *Paul: The Theology of the Apostle in the Light of Jewish Religious History*. Translated by H. Knight. Philadelphia: Westminster, 1961.

Schrenk, G., and G. Quell. "πατήρ κτλ." In *Theological Dictionary of the New Testament*, 5:945–1022. Grand Rapids: Eerdmans, 1964–1976.

Schweitzer, A. *The Mysticism of Paul the Apostle.* Translated by W. Montgomery. London: Black, 1931.

Tannehill, R. C. *Dying and Rising with Christ.* Beihefte zur Zeitschrift für die neutestamentliche Wissenschaft 32. Berlin: Töpelmann, 1967.

Thielman, F. *From Plight to Solution: A Jewish Framework for Understanding Paul's View of the Law in Galatians and Romans.* Novum Testamentum Supplements. Leiden: Brill, 1989.

Westerholm, S. *Perspectives Old and New on Paul: The "Lutheran" Paul and His Critics.* Grand Rapids/Cambridge, Eng.: Eerdmans, 2004.

Wikenhauser, A. *Pauline Mysticism: Christ in the Mystical Teaching of St. Paul.* Translated by J. Cunningham. Freiburg: Herder; Edinburgh: Nelson, 1960.

Williams, S. K. "Again *Pistis Christou.*" *Catholic Biblical Quarterly* 49 (1987): 431–47.

Commentaries on Romans

Barrett, C. K. *A Commentary on the Epistle to the Romans.* Harper's New Testament Commentaries. New York: Harper & Row, 1957.

Cranfield, C. E. B. *A Critical and Exegetical Commentary on the Epistle to the Romans.* 2 vols. International Critical Commentary. Edinburgh: Clark, 1975–1979.

Dodd, C. H. *The Epistle of Paul to the Romans.* Moffatt New Testament Commentary. London: Hodder & Stoughton, 1932.

Dunn, J. D. G. *Romans.* 2 vols. Word Biblical Commentary 38. Dallas: Word, 1988.

Fitzmyer, J. A. *Romans.* Anchor Bible 33. New York: Doubleday, 1993.

Käsemann, E. *Commentary on Romans.* Translated by G. W. Bromiley. Grand Rapids: Eerdmans, 1980.

Morris, L. *The Epistle to the Romans.* Grand Rapids: Eerdmans, 1988.